THE CRYPT

HandBook

A GUIDE TO START MINING
CRYPTOCURRENCY TODAY!

"Why buy it when you can mine it?" -

Daniel Rivera
AKA Lets Mine Coins

Lowry Global Media LLC

The Crypto Miners Handbook, A Guide to Start Mining Cryptocurrency Today! Lets Mine Coins

Copyright © by Lowry Global Media LLC

Disclaimer
The purpose of this book is to provide the public with information. This information should not constitute "financial advice", "legal advice", or "investment advice". Please consult your financial advisor, or a licensed professional for advice tailored to your financial needs and objectives.

ISBN: 978-1-950961-71-9

TABLE OF CONTENTS

Introduction

This guide has been carefully assembled from open-sources to help you gain the knowledge necessary to efficiently mine cryptocurrency. The information in this guide will give you an in-depth look at the crypto mining space and rundown on the components needed for mining cryptocurrency today.

Daniel Rivera, AKA "Lets Mine Coins" on YouTube, has many years of experience and is a master at GPU mining. Daniel's knowledge about building and running mining rigs will give you a major advantage when making important decisions about your crypto mining rigs.

As you read through this book and learn more about mining cryptocurrency, and also watch Daniel's crypto mining videos on YouTube, you will begin to gain a deeper understanding of how to build highly stable and very profitable mining rigs!

You have made the decision to invest in yourself and use some of the most groundbreaking technology our generation has ever seen. Thank you for purchasing this book, Daniel wishes you the best of luck along your crypto mining journey.

Search "Lets Mine Coins" on YouTube for up to date content.

Section 1

Cryptocurrency Mining

In cryptocurrency networks, *mining* is a validation of transactions. For this effort, successful miners obtain new cryptocurrency as a reward. The reward decreases transaction fees by creating a complementary incentive to contribute to the processing power of the network. The rate of generating hashes, which validate any transaction, has been increased by the use of specialized machines such as FPGAs and ASICs running complex hashing algorithms like SHA-256 and scrypt.[39] This arms race for cheaper-yet-efficient machines has existed since the day the first cryptocurrency, bitcoin, was introduced in 2009.[39] With more people venturing into the world of virtual currency, generating hashes for this validation has become far more complex over the years, with miners having to invest large sums of money on employing multiple high performance ASICs. Thus the value of the currency obtained for finding a hash often does not justify the amount of money spent on setting up the machines, the cooling facilities to overcome the heat they produce, and the electricity required to run them.[40] As of July 2019, bitcoin's electricity consumption is estimated to about 7 gigawatts, 0.2% of the global total, or equivalent to that of Switzerland.[41]

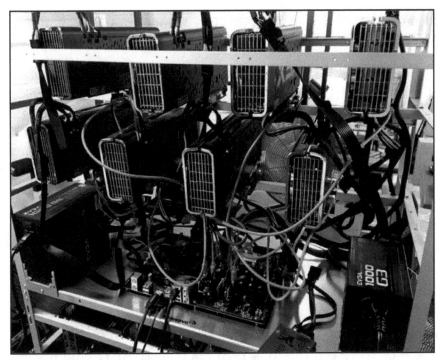

Cryptocurrency Mining Rig

Some miners pool resources, sharing their processing power over a network to split the reward equally, according to the amount of work they contributed to the probability of finding a block. A "share" is awarded to members of the mining pool who present a valid partial proof-of-work.

As of February 2018, the Chinese Government halted trading of virtual currency, banned initial coin offerings and shut down mining. Some Chinese miners have since relocated to Canada.[42] One company is operating data centers for mining operations at Canadian oil and gas field sites, due to low gas prices.[43] In June 2018, Hydro Quebec proposed to the provincial government to allocate 500 MW to crypto companies for mining.[44] According to a February 2018 report from *Fortune*,[45] Iceland has become a haven for cryptocurrency miners in part because of its cheap electricity.

In March 2018, the city of Plattsburgh in upstate New York put an 18-month moratorium on all cryptocurrency mining in an effort to preserve natural resources and the "character and direction" of the city.[46]

Cryptocurrency, GPU Price Rise

An increase in cryptocurrency mining increased the demand for graphics cards (GPU) in 2017.[47] (The computing power of GPUs makes them well-suited to generating hashes.) Popular favorites of cryptocurrency miners such as Nvidia's GTX 1060 and GTX 1070 graphics cards, as well as AMD's RX 570 and RX 580 GPUs, doubled or tripled in price – or were out of stock.[48] A GTX 1070 Ti which was released at a price of $450 sold for as much as $1100. Another popular card GTX 1060's 6 GB model was released at an MSRP of $250, sold for almost $500. RX 570 and RX 580 cards from AMD were out of stock for almost a year. Miners regularly buy up the entire stock of new GPU's as soon as they are available.[49]

Nvidia has asked retailers to do what they can when it comes to selling GPUs to gamers instead of miners. "Gamers come first for Nvidia," said Boris Böhles, PR manager for Nvidia in the German region.[50]

Cryptocurrency, Block Rewards

Proof-of-work cryptocurrencies, such as bitcoin, offer block rewards incentives for miners. There has been an implicit belief that whether miners are paid by block rewards or transaction fees does not affect the security of the blockchain, but a study suggests that this may not be the case under certain circumstances.[54]

The rewards paid to miners increase the supply of the cryptocurrency. By making sure that verifying transactions is a costly business, the integrity of the network can be preserved as long as benevolent nodes control a majority of computing power. The verification algorithm requires a lot of processing power, and thus electricity in order to make verification costly enough to accurately validate public blockchain. Not only do miners have to factor in the costs associated with expensive equipment necessary to stand a chance of solving a hash problem, they further must consider the significant amount of electrical power in search of the solution. Generally, the block rewards outweigh electricity and equipment costs, but this may not always be the case.[55]

The current value, not the long-term value, of the cryptocurrency supports the reward scheme to incentivize miners to engage in costly mining activities. Some sources claim that the current bitcoin design is very inefficient, generating a welfare loss of 1.4% relative to an efficient cash system. The main source for this inefficiency is the large mining cost, which is estimated to be 360 Million USD per year. This translates into users being willing to accept a cash system with an inflation rate of 230% before being better off using bitcoin as a means of payment. However, the efficiency of the bitcoin system can be significantly improved by optimizing the rate of coin creation and minimizing transaction fees. Another potential improvement is to eliminate inefficient mining activities by changing the consensus protocol altogether.[56]

Cryptocurrency, Transaction Fees

Transaction fees for cryptocurrency depend mainly on the supply of network capacity at the time, versus the demand from the currency holder for a faster transaction.[*citation needed*] The currency holder can choose a specific transaction fee, while network entities process transactions in order of highest offered fee to lowest.[*citation needed*] Cryptocurrency exchanges can simplify the process for currency holders by offering priority alternatives and thereby determine which fee will likely cause the transaction to be processed in the requested time.[*citation needed*]

For ether, transaction fees differ by computational complexity, bandwidth use, and storage needs, while bitcoin transaction fees differ by transaction size and whether the transaction uses SegWit. In September 2018, the median transaction fee for ether corresponded to $0.017,[57] while for bitcoin it corresponded to $0.55.[58]

Some cryptocurrencies have no transaction fees, and instead rely on client-side proof-of-work as the transaction prioritization and anti-spam mechanism.[59][60][61]

Mining Pool

In the context of cryptocurrency mining, a **mining pool** is the pooling of resources by miners, who share their processing power over a network, to split the reward equally, according to the amount of work they contributed to the probability of finding a block. A "share" is awarded to members of the mining pool who present a valid partial proof-of-work. Mining in pools began when the difficulty for mining increased to the point where it could take centuries for slower miners to generate a block. The solution to this problem was for miners to pool their resources so they could generate blocks more quickly and therefore receive a portion of the block reward on a consistent basis, rather than randomly once every few years. [1][2][3]

Mining Pool, Brief History

- **Late 2010:** Slush launched the first mining pool
- **2011–2013:** The era of deepbit, which at its peak, shares up to 45% of the network hashrate
- **2013–2014:** Since the introduction of ASIC, and when deepbit failed to support the newer stratum protocol, GHash.IO replaced deepbit and became the largest
- **2014–2015:** Rise of China. F2Pool which launched in May 2013, replaced GHash.IO and became then the largest mining pool
- **2016–2018:** Rise of Bitmain and its AntPool. Bitmain

also controls a few other smaller pools like BTC.com and ViaBTC

- **2019–2020:** The launch of Poolin. Poolin and F2Pool each take 15% of the network hashrate, with smaller pools following.
- **2020:** Binance launches a mining pool following Huobi and OKex. Luxor launches a US-based mining pool.

Dan's Pro Tip: "Some of my favorite pools are: Ethermine, Nanopool, and Flexpool. Watch my YouTube videos for more information about mining pools."

Mining Pool, Mining Pool Share

Share is the principal concept of the mining pool operation. Share is a potential block solution. So it may be a block solution, but it is not necessarily so. For example, suppose a block solution is a number that ends with 10 zeros and, a share may be a number with 5 zeros at the end. Sooner or later one of the shares will have not only 5, but 10 zeros at the end, and this will be the block solution.

Mining pools need shares to estimate the miner's contribution to the work performed by the pool to find a block. There are numerous miner reward systems: PPS, PROP, PPLNS, PPLNT, and many more.

Mining Pool, Mining Pool Methods, Pay-per-Share

The Pay-per-Share (PPS) approach offers an instant, guaranteed payout to a miner for his contribution to the probability that the pool finds a block. Miners are paid out from the pool's existing balance and can withdraw their payout immediately. This model allows for the least possible variance in payment for miners while also transferring much of the risk to the pool's operator.

Mining Pool, Mining Pool Methods, Bitcoin Pooled Mining

Bitcoin Pooled mining (BPM), also known as "slush's system", due to its first use on a pool called "slush's pool', uses a system where older shares from the beginning of a block round are given less weight than more recent shares. A new round starts the moment the pool solves a block and miners are rewarded **Proportional** to the shares submitted. [5] This reduces the ability to cheat the mining pool system by switching pools during a round, to maximize profit.

Mining Pool, Mining Pool Methods, Pay-per-last-N-shares

Pay-per-last-N-shares (PPLNS) method is similar to **Proportional**, but the miner's reward is calculated on a basis of N last shares, instead of all shares for the last round. It means that when a block is found, the reward of each miner is calculated based on the miner contribution to the last N pool shares. Therefore, if the round was short enough all miners get more profit and vice versa.

Mining Pool, Mining Pool Methods, Solo Mining Pool

Solo pools operate the same way as usual pools, with the only difference being that block reward is not distributed among all miners. The entire reward in a solo pool goes to the miner who finds the block.

Mining Pool, Mining Pool Methods, Peer-to-Peer Mining Pool

Peer-to-peer mining pool (P2Pool) decentralizes the responsibilities of a pool server, removing the chance of the pool operator cheating or the server being a single point of failure. Miners work on a side blockchain called a share chain, mining at a lower difficulty at a rate of one share block per 30 seconds. Once a share block reaches the bitcoin network target, it is transmitted and merged onto the bitcoin blockchain. Miners are rewarded when this occurs proportional to the shares submitted prior to the target block. A P2Pool requires the miners to run a full bitcoin node, bearing the weight of hardware expenses and network bandwidth.[5][6]

Mining Pool, Mining Pool Methods, Geometric Method

Geometric Method (GM) was invented by Meni Rosenfeld. [7] It is based on the same "score" idea, as Slush's method: the score granted for every new share, relatively to already existing score and the score of future shares, is always the same, thus there is no advantage to mining early or late in the round.

Mining Pool, Transaction Fees

Usually, the blocks in the cryptocurrency network contain transactions. Transaction fees are paid to the miner (mining pool). Different mining pools could share these fees between their miners or not. Pay-per-last-N-shares (PPLNS), Pay-Per-Share Plus (PPS+) or Full Pay-Per-Share (FPPS) are the most fair methods where the payouts from the pool include not only the block subsidy but also the transaction fees.

Mining Pool, Multipool Mining

Multipools switch between different altcoins and constantly calculate which coin is at that moment the most profitable to mine. Two key factors are involved in the algorithm that calculates profitability, the block time, and the price on the exchanges. To avoid the need for many different wallets for all possible minable coins, multipools may automatically exchange the mined coin to a coin that is accepted in the mainstream (for example bitcoin). Using this method, because the most profitable coins are being mined and then sold for the intended coin, it is possible to receive more coins in the intended currency than by mining that currency alone. This method also increases demand on the intended coin, which has the side effect of increasing or stabilizing the value of the intended coin.[8]

Some companies that sell hash power may do so by aggregating the work of many small miners (for example, NiceHash), paying them proportionally by share like a pool would. Some such companies operate their own pools. These can be considered multipools, because they usually employ a similar method of work switching, although the work they assign is determined by customer demand rather than "raw" profitability.

Bitcoin Network, Mining

To form a distributed timestamp server as a peer-to-peer network, bitcoin uses a proof-of-work system.[3] This work is often called *bitcoin mining*.

Requiring a proof of work to accept a new block to the blockchain was Satoshi Nakamoto's key innovation. The mining process involves identifying a block that, when hashed twice with SHA-256, yields a number smaller than the given difficulty target. While the average work required increases in inverse proportion to the difficulty target, a hash can always be verified by executing a single round of double SHA-256.

For the bitcoin timestamp network, a valid proof of work is found by incrementing a nonce until a value is found that gives the block's hash the required number of leading zero bits. Once the hashing has produced a valid result, the block cannot be changed without redoing the work. As later blocks are chained after it, the work to change the block would include redoing the work for each subsequent block.

Majority consensus in bitcoin is represented by the longest chain, which required the greatest amount of effort to produce. If a majority of computing power is controlled by honest nodes, the honest chain will grow fastest and outpace any competing chains. To modify a past block, an attacker would have to redo the proof-of-work of that block and all blocks after it and then surpass the work of the honest nodes. The probability of a slower attacker catching up diminishes exponentially as subsequent blocks are added. [3]

To compensate for increasing hardware speed and varying interest in running nodes over time, the difficulty of finding a valid hash is adjusted roughly every two weeks. If blocks are generated too quickly, the difficulty increases and more hashes are required to make a block and to generate new bitcoins.[3]

Bitcoin Network, Mining, Difficulty

Bitcoin mining is a competitive endeavor. An "arms race" has been observed through the various hashing technologies that have been used to mine bitcoins: basic CPUs, high-end GPUs common in many gaming computers, FPGAs and ASICs all have been used, each reducing the profitability of the less-specialized technology. Bitcoin-specific ASICs are now the primary method of mining bitcoin and have surpassed GPU speed by as much as 300-fold. The difficulty within the mining process involves self-adjusting to the network's accumulated mining power. As bitcoins have become more difficult to mine, computer hardware manufacturing companies have seen an increase in sales of high-end ASIC products.[4]

Computing power is often bundled together or "pooled" to reduce variance in miner income. Individual mining rigs often have to wait for long periods to confirm a block of transactions and receive payment. In a pool, all participating miners get paid every time a participating server solves a block. This payment depends on the amount of work an individual miner contributed to help find that block.[5]

Proof of Work

Proof of work (PoW) is a form of cryptographic zero-knowledge proof in which one party (the *prover*) proves to others (the *verifiers*) that a certain amount of computational effort has been expended for some purpose. Verifiers can subsequently confirm this expenditure with minimal effort on their part. The concept was invented by Cynthia Dwork and Moni Naor in 1993 as a way to deter denial-of-service attacks and other service abuses such as spam on a network by requiring some work from a service requester, usually meaning processing time by a computer. The term "proof of work" was first coined and formalized in a 1999 paper by

Markus Jakobsson and Ari Juels.[1][2] Proof of work was later popularized by Bitcoin as a foundation for consensus in permissionless blockchains and cryptocurrencies, in which miners compete to append blocks and mint new currency, each miner experiencing a success probability proportional to their computational effort provably expended. PoW and PoS (Proof of Stake) are the two best known consensus mechanisms. In the context of cryptocurrencies they are the most common mechanisms.[3]

A key feature of proof-of-work schemes is their asymmetry: the work must be moderately hard (yet feasible) on the prover or requester side but easy to check for the verifier or service provider. This idea is also known as a CPU cost function, client puzzle, computational puzzle, or CPU pricing function. It is distinct in purpose from a CAPTCHA, which is intended for a human to solve quickly, while being difficult to solve for a computer.

Proof of Work, Background

One popular system, used in Hashcash, uses partial hash inversions to prove that work was done, as a goodwill token to send an e-mail. For instance, the following header represents about 2^{52} hash computations to send a message to calvin@comics.net on January 19, 2038:

X-Hashcash:
```
1:52:380119:calvin@comics.net:::9B760005
E92F0DAE
```

It is verified with a single computation by checking that the SHA-1 hash of the stamp (omit the header name X-

Hashcash: including the colon and any amount of whitespace following it up to the digit '1') begins with 52 binary zeros, that is 13 hexadecimal zeros:[1]

```
0000000000000756af69e2ffbdb930261873cd71
```

Whether PoW systems can actually solve a particular denial-of-service issue such as the spam problem is subject to debate;[4][5] the system must make sending spam emails obtrusively unproductive for the spammer, but should also not prevent legitimate users from sending their messages. In other words, a genuine user should not encounter any difficulties when sending an email, but an email spammer would have to expend a considerable amount of computing power to send out many emails at once. Proof-of-work systems are being used as a primitive by other more complex cryptographic systems such as bitcoin which uses a system similar to Hashcash.

Proof of Work, Variants

There are two classes of proof-of-work protocols.

- **Challenge–response** protocols assume a direct interactive link between the requester (client) and the provider (server). The provider chooses a challenge, say an item in a set with a property, the requester finds the relevant response in the set, which is sent back and checked by the provider. As the challenge is chosen on the spot by the provider, its difficulty can be adapted to its current load. The work on the requester side may be bounded if the challenge-response protocol has a known solution (chosen by the provider), or is known to exist within a bounded search space.

- **Solution–verification** protocols do not assume such a link: as a result, the problem must be self-imposed before a solution is sought by the requester, and the provider must check both the problem choice and the found solution. Most such schemes are unbounded probabilistic iterative procedures such as Hashcash.

Known-solution protocols tend to have slightly lower variance than unbounded probabilistic protocols because the variance of a rectangular distribution is lower than the variance of a Poisson distribution (with the same mean). [*further explanation needed*] A generic technique for reducing variance is to use multiple independent sub-challenges, as the average of multiple samples will have a lower variance.

There are also fixed-cost functions such as the time-lock puzzle.

Moreover, the underlying functions used by these schemes may be:

- **CPU-bound** where the computation runs at the speed of the processor, which greatly varies in time, as well as from high-end server to low-end portable devices. [6]
- **Memory-bound**[7][8][9][10] where the computation speed is bound by main memory accesses (either latency or bandwidth), the performance of which is expected to be less sensitive to hardware evolution.
- **Network-bound**[11] if the client must perform few computations, but must collect some tokens from

remote servers before querying the final service provider. In this sense, the work is not actually performed by the requester, but it incurs delays anyway because of the latency to get the required tokens.

Finally, some PoW systems offer **shortcut** computations that allow participants who know a secret, typically a private key, to generate cheap PoWs. The rationale is that mailing-list holders may generate stamps for every recipient without incurring a high cost. Whether such a feature is desirable depends on the usage scenario.

Proof of Work, Reusable Proof-of-work as E-money

Computer scientist Hal Finney built on the proof-of-work idea, yielding a system that exploited reusable proof of work (RPoW).[19] The idea of making proofs of work reusable for some practical purpose had already been established in 1999.[1] Finney's purpose for RPoW was as token money. Just as a gold coin's value is thought to be underpinned by the value of the raw gold needed to make it, the value of an RPoW token is guaranteed by the value of the real-world resources required to 'mint' a PoW token. In Finney's version of RPoW, the PoW token is a piece of Hashcash.

A website can demand a PoW token in exchange for service. Requiring a PoW token from users would inhibit frivolous or excessive use of the service, sparing the service's underlying resources, such as bandwidth to the

Internet, computation, disk space, electricity, and administrative overhead.

Finney's RPoW system differed from a PoW system in permitting the random exchange of tokens without repeating the work required to generate them. After someone had "spent" a PoW token at a website, the website's operator could exchange that "spent" PoW token for a new, unspent RPoW token, which could then be spent at some third-party website similarly equipped to accept RPoW tokens. This would save the resources otherwise needed to 'mint' a PoW token. The anti-counterfeit property of the RPoW token was guaranteed by remote attestation. The RPoW server that exchanges a used PoW or RPoW token for a new one of equal value uses remote attestation to allow any interested party to verify what software is running on the RPoW server. Since the source code for Finney's RPoW software was published (under a BSD-like license), any sufficiently knowledgeable programmer could, by inspecting the code, verify that the software (and, by extension, the RPoW server) never issued a new token except in exchange for a spent token of equal value.

Until 2009, Finney's system was the only RPoW system to have been implemented; it never saw economically significant use.

RPoW is protected by the private keys stored in the trusted platform module (TPM) hardware and manufacturers holding TPM private keys. Stealing a TPM manufacturer's key or obtaining the key by examining the TPM chip itself would subvert that assurance.

Proof of Work, Reusable Proof-of-work as E-money, Bitcoin-type Proof of Work

In 2009, the Bitcoin network went online. Bitcoin is a proof-of-work cryptocurrency that, like Finney's RPoW, is also based on the Hashcash PoW. But in Bitcoin, double-spend protection is provided by a decentralized P2P protocol for tracking transfers of coins, rather than the hardware trusted computing function used by RPoW. Bitcoin has better trustworthiness because it is protected by computation. Bitcoins are "mined" using the Hashcash proof-of-work function by individual miners and verified by the decentralized nodes in the P2P bitcoin network.

The difficulty is periodically adjusted to keep the block time around a target time.

Proof of Work, Reusable Proof-of-work as E-money, Energy Consumption

Since the creation of Bitcoin, proof-of-work has been the predominant design of peer-to-peer cryptocurrency. Many studies have been looking at the energy consumption of mining.[20] The PoW mechanism requires a vast amount of computing resources, which consume a significant amount of electricity. Bitcoin's energy consumption can power an entire country.[3]

However, there is no alternative design known that could replace proof-of-work but keeps its desirable attributes such as:[*citation needed*]

- permissionless mining

- fair distribution of coins
- security against many known attacks
- bootstrappability of new nodes in a hostile environment
- graceful degradation and recovery even in the face of a successful attack or network failure
- unforgeable and statically verifiable costliness

Also, there have been many attempts at making proof-of-work use non-specialist hardware. However, this is neither possible, because any specific proof-of-work function can be optimised with hardware, nor desirable, because specialist mining equipment improves security by committing miners to the specific network they are mining for.[*citation needed*]

Proof of Work, ASICs and Mining Pools

Within the Bitcoin community there are groups working together in mining pools.[21] Some miners use application-specific integrated circuits (ASICs) for PoW.[22] This trend toward mining pools and specialized ASICs has made mining some cryptocurrencies economically infeasible for most players without access to the latest ASICs, nearby sources of inexpensive energy, or other special advantages. [23]

Some PoWs claim to be ASIC-resistant, i.e. to limit the efficiency gain that an ASIC can have over commodity hardware, like a GPU, to be well under an order of magnitude. ASIC resistance has the advantage of keeping mining economically feasible on commodity hardware, but also contributes to the corresponding risk that an attacker can briefly rent access to a large amount of unspecialized commodity processing power to launch a 51% attack against a cryptocurrency.[24]

Proof of Stake

Proof of stake (PoS) is a type of consensus mechanisms by which a cryptocurrency blockchain network achieves distributed consensus. In PoS-based cryptocurrencies the creator of the next block is chosen via various combinations of random selection and wealth or age (*i.e.*, the stake).

Proof of Stake, PoS vs PoW

A consensus mechanism can be structured in a number of ways. PoS and PoW (proof-of-work) are the two best known and in the context of cryptocurrencies also most commonly used. Incentives differ between the two systems of block generation. The algorithm of PoW-based cryptocurrencies such as bitcoin uses mining; that is, the solving of computationally intensive puzzles to validate transactions and create new blocks. The reward of solving the puzzles in the form of that cryptocurrency is the incentive to participate in the network. The PoW mechanism requires a vast amount of computing resources, which consume a significant amount of electricity. With PoS there is no need for 'hard Work'. Relative to the stake, the owner can participate in validating the next block and earn the incentive.[1]

Proof of Stake, Block Selection Variants

Proof of stake must have a way of defining the next valid block in any blockchain. Selection by account balance would result in (undesirable) centralization, as the single richest member would have a permanent advantage. Instead, several different methods of selection have been devised.

Proof of Stake, Block Selection Variants, Coin Age-based Selection

Peercoin's proof-of-stake system combines randomization with the concept of "coin age", a number derived from the product of the number of coins multiplied by the number of days the coins have been held.

Coins that have been unspent for at least 30 days begin competing for the next block. Older and larger sets of coins have a greater probability of signing the next block. However, once a stake of coins has been used to sign a block, it must start over with zero "coin age" and thus wait at least 30 more days before signing another block. Also, the probability of finding the next block reaches a maximum after 90 days in order to prevent very old or very large collections of stakes from dominating the blockchain. [2][*non-primary source needed*]

This process secures the network and gradually produces

new coins over time without consuming significant computational power.[3][*unreliable source?*]

Proof of Stake, Criticism

Some authors[4][*non-primary source needed*][5][*non-primary source needed*] argue that proof of stake is not an ideal option for a distributed consensus protocol. One issue that can arise is the "nothing-at-stake" problem, wherein block generators have nothing to lose by voting for multiple blockchain histories, thereby preventing consensus from being achieved. Because unlike in proof-of-work systems, there is little cost to working on several chains.[6] Some cryptocurrencies are vulnerable to Fake Stake attacks, where an attacker uses no or very little stake to crash an affected node.[7]

Notable attempts to solve these problems include:

- Peercoin is the first cryptocurrency that applied the concept of PoS.[*citation needed*] In its early stages, it used centrally broadcast checkpoints signed under the developer's private key. No blockchain reorganization was allowed deeper than the last known checkpoints. Checkpoints are opt-in as of v0.6 and are not enforced now that the network has reached a suitable level of distribution.[*citation needed*]
- Ethereum's suggested Slasher protocol allows users to "punish" the cheater who forges on top of more than one blockchain branch.[8][*non-primary source needed*] This proposal assumes that one must double-sign to create a fork and that one can be punished for creating a fork while not having stake. However,

Slasher was never adopted; Ethereum developers concluded proof of stake is "non-trivial",[9] opting instead to adopt a proof-of-work algorithm named Ethash.[10][*non-primary source needed*]

- Nxt's protocol only allows reorganization of the last 720 blocks.[11][*non-primary source needed*] However, this merely rescales the problem: a client may follow a fork of 721 blocks, regardless of whether it is the tallest blockchain, thereby preventing consensus.

Application-specific Integrated Circuit (ASIC)

An **application-specific integrated circuit (ASIC)** is an integrated circuit (IC) chip customized for a particular use, rather than intended for general-purpose use. For example, a chip designed to run in a digital voice recorder or a high-efficiency bitcoin miner is an ASIC. Application-specific standard product (ASSP) chips are intermediate between ASICs and industry standard integrated circuits like the 7400 series or the 4000 series.[1] ASIC chips are typically fabricated using metal-oxide-semiconductor (MOS) technology, as MOS integrated circuit chips.[2]

As feature sizes have shrunk and design tools improved over the years, the maximum complexity (and hence functionality) possible in an ASIC has grown from 5,000 logic gates to over 100 million. Modern ASICs often include entire microprocessors, memory blocks including ROM, RAM, EEPROM, flash memory and other large building blocks. Such an ASIC is often termed a SoC (system-on-chip).

Dan's Pro Tip: "ASICS should only be bought if you are investing on a business level scale. My recommendation will be focused on GPU rigs."

Graphics Processing Unit (GPU)

A **graphics processing unit (GPU)** is a specialized electronic circuit designed to rapidly manipulate and alter memory to accelerate the creation of images in a frame buffer intended for output to a display device. GPUs are used in embedded systems, mobile phones, personal computers, workstations, and game consoles. Modern GPUs are very efficient at manipulating computer graphics and image processing. Their highly parallel structure makes them more efficient than general-purpose central processing units (CPUs) for algorithms that process large blocks of data in parallel. In a personal computer, a GPU can be present on a video card or embedded on the motherboard. In certain CPUs, they are embedded on the CPU die.[1]

Dan's Pro Tip: "Gpu's will be the bulk and most important part of your investment! Be sure you are buying the most efficient cards you can find at the time and at the most reasonable price. Refer my YouTube videos for recommendations."

Graphics Processing Unit (GPU), Computational Functions

Modern GPUs use most of their transistors to do calculations related to 3D computer graphics. In addition to the 3D hardware, today's GPUs include basic 2D acceleration and framebuffer capabilities (usually with a VGA compatibility mode). Newer cards such as AMD/ATI HD5000-HD7000 even lack 2D acceleration; it has to be emulated by 3D hardware. GPUs were initially used to accelerate the memory-intensive work of texture mapping and rendering polygons, later adding units to accelerate geometric calculations such as the rotation and translation of vertices into different coordinate systems. Recent developments in GPUs include support for programmable shaders which can manipulate vertices and textures with many of the same operations supported by CPUs, oversampling and interpolation techniques to reduce aliasing, and very high-precision color spaces. Because most of these computations involve matrix and vector operations, engineers and scientists have increasingly studied the use of GPUs for non-graphical calculations; like for mining cryptocurrencies.

Cryptocurrency Wallet

Dan's Pro Tip: "A hardware wallet such as Ledger Nano is a priority! This is the safest way to keep your funds protected from hackers. Be sure to store your private keys in cold storage and are not accessible by the internet."

A **cryptocurrency wallet** is a device,[1] physical medium, [2] program or a service which stores the public and/or private keys[3] for cryptocurrency transactions. In addition to this basic function of storing the keys, a cryptocurrency wallet more often also offers the functionality of encrypting and/or signing information. Signing can for example result in executing a smart contract, a cryptocurrency transaction (see "bitcoin transaction" image), identification or legally signing a 'document' (see "application form" image).[4]

Cryptocurrency Wallet, Characteristics

In addition to the basic function of storing the keys, a cryptocurrency wallet may also have one or more of the following characteristics.

Cryptocurrency Wallet, Characteristics, Simple Cryptocurrency Wallet

A simple cryptocurrency wallet contains pairs of public and private cryptographic keys. The keys can be used to track ownership, receive or spend cryptocurrencies.[5] A public key allows others to make payments to the address derived from it, whereas a private key enables the spending of cryptocurrency from that address.[6]

The cryptocurrency itself is not in the wallet. In the case of bitcoin and cryptocurrencies derived from it, the cryptocurrency is decentrally stored and maintained in a publicly available distributed ledger called the *blockchain*. [5]

Cryptocurrency Wallet, Characteristics, eID Wallet

Some wallets are specifically designed to be compatible with a framework. The European Union is creating an eIDAS compatible European Self-Sovereign Identity Framework (ESSIF) which runs on the European Blockchain Services Infrastructure (EBSI). The EBSI wallet is designed to (securely) provide information, an eID and to sign 'transactions'.[4]

Cryptocurrency Wallet, Characteristics, Multisignature Wallet

In contrast to simple cryptocurrency wallets requiring just one party to sign a transaction, multisignature wallets require multiple parties to sign a transaction.[7] Multisignature wallets are designed to have increased security.[8]

Cryptocurrency Wallet, Characteristics, Smart Contract

In the cryptocurrency space, smart contracts are digitally signed in the same way a cryptocurrency transaction is signed. The signing keys are held in a cryptocurrency wallet.

Cryptocurrency Wallet, Characteristics, Key Derivation, Deterministic Wallet

With a deterministic wallet a single key can be used to generate an entire tree of key pairs.[9] This single key serves as the root of the tree. The generated mnemonic sentence or word seed is simply a more human-readable way of expressing the key used as the root, as it can be algorithmically converted into the root private key. Those words, in that order, will always generate exactly the same root key. A word phrase could consist of 24 words like: begin friend black earth beauty praise pride refuse horror believe relief gospel end destroy champion build better awesome. That single root key is not replacing all other private keys, but rather is being used to generate them. All the addresses still have different private keys, but they can all be restored by that single root key. The private keys to every address it has and will ever give out in the future can be recalculated given the root key. That root key, in turn, can be recalculated by feeding in the word seed. The mnemonic sentence is the backup of the wallet. If a wallet supports the same (mnemonic sentence) technique, then the backup can also be restored on another software or hardware wallet.

A mnemonic sentence is considered secure. The BIP-39 standard creates a 512-bit seed from any given mnemonic. The set of possible wallets is 2^{512}. Every passphrase leads to a valid wallet. If the wallet was not previously used it will be empty.[5]:104

Cryptocurrency Wallet, Characteristics, Key Derivation, Non-deterministic Wallet

In a non-deterministic wallet, each key is randomly generated on its own accord, and they are not seeded from a common key. Therefore, any backups of the wallet must store each and every single private key used as an address, as well as a buffer of 100 or so future keys that may have already been given out as addresses but not received payments yet.[5]:94

Cryptocurrency Wallet, Characteristics, Wallet Access

When choosing a wallet, the owner must keep in mind who is supposed to have access to (a copy of) the private keys and thus potentially has signing capabilities. In case of cryptocurrency the user needs to trust the provider to keep the cryptocurrency safe, just like with a bank. Trust was misplaced in the case of the Mt. Gox exchange, which 'lost' most of their clients' bitcoins. Downloading a cryptocurrency wallet from a wallet provider to a computer or phone does not automatically mean that the owner is the only one who has a copy of the private keys. For example, with Coinbase, it is possible to install a wallet on a phone and to also have access to the same wallet through their website. A wallet can also have known or unknown vulnerabilities. A supply chain attack or side-channel attack are ways of a vulnerability introduction. In extreme cases even a computer which is not connected to any network can be hacked.[10] For receiving cryptocurrency, access to the receiving wallet is not needed. The sending party only needs to know the destination address. Anyone can send cryptocurrency to an address. Only the one who has the private key of the corresponding (public key) address can use it.

Section 2
Mining Rig Components

Mining Rig Components, Motherboard

A **motherboard** (also called **mainboard**, main **circuit board, system board, baseboard, planar board, logic board**,[1] or **mobo**) is the main printed circuit board (PCB) in general-purpose computers and other expandable systems. It holds and allows communication between many of the crucial electronic components of a system, such as the central processing unit (CPU) and memory, and provides connectors for other peripherals. Unlike a backplane, a motherboard usually contains significant sub-systems, such as the central processor, the chipset's input/output and memory controllers, interface connectors, and other components integrated for general use.

Motherboard for a Mining Rig.

Motherboard means specifically a PCB with expansion capabilities. As the name suggests, this board is often referred to as the "mother" of all components attached to it, which often include peripherals, interface cards, and daughtercards: sound cards, video cards, network cards, host bus adapters, IEEE 1394 cards; and a variety of other custom components.

Mining Rig Components, Central Processing Unit (CPU)

A **central processing unit (CPU)**, also called a **central processor, main processor** or just **processor,** is the electronic circuitry within a computer that executes instructions that make up a computer program. The CPU performs basic arithmetic, logic, controlling, and input/output (I/O) operations specified by the instructions in the program. This contrasts with external components such as main memory and I/O circuitry,[1] and specialized processors such as graphics processing units (GPUs).

The computer industry used the term "central processing unit" as early as 1955.[2][3]

CPU for a Mining Rig.

The form, design, and implementation of CPUs have changed over time, but their fundamental operation remains almost unchanged. Principal components of a CPU include the arithmetic logic unit (ALU) that performs arithmetic and logic operations, processor registers that supply operands to the ALU and store the results of ALU operations, and a control unit that orchestrates the fetching (from memory) and execution of instructions by directing the coordinated operations of the ALU, registers and other components.

Most modern CPUs are implemented on integrated circuit (IC) microprocessors, with one or more CPUs on a single metal-oxide-semiconductor (MOS) IC chip. Microprocessors chips with multiple CPUs are multi-core processors. The individual physical CPUs, **processor cores**, can also be multithreaded to create additional virtual or logical CPUs.[4]

Mining Rig Components, Random-access Memory (RAM)

Random-access memory (RAM) is a form of computer memory that can be read and changed in any order, typically used to store working data and machine code.[1] [2] A random-access memory device allows data items to be read or written in almost the same amount of time irrespective of the physical location of data inside the memory. In contrast, with other direct-access data storage media such as hard disks, CD-RWs, DVD-RWs and the older magnetic tapes and drum memory, the time required to read and write data items varies significantly depending on their physical locations on the recording medium, due to mechanical limitations such as media rotation speeds and arm movement.

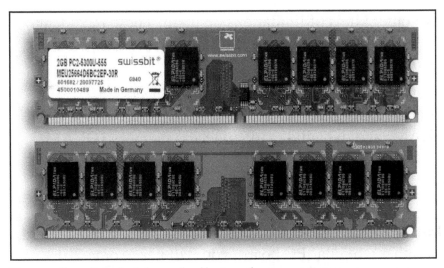

Example of writable volatile random-access memory:
Synchronous Dynamic RAM modules, primarily used as
main memory in personal computers, workstations, and
servers.

RAM contains multiplexing and demultiplexing circuitry, to
connect the data lines to the addressed storage for reading
or writing the entry. Usually more than one bit of storage is
accessed by the same address, and RAM devices often have
multiple data lines and are said to be "8-bit" or "16-bit", etc.
devices.

In today's technology, random-access memory takes the
form of integrated circuit (IC) chips with MOS (metal-
oxide-semiconductor) memory cells. RAM is normally
associated with volatile types of memory (such as dynamic
random-access memory (DRAM) modules), where stored
information is lost if power is removed, although non-
volatile RAM has also been developed.[3] Other types of
non-volatile memories exist that allow random access for
read operations, but either do not allow write operations or

have other kinds of limitations on them. These include most types of ROM and a type of flash memory called *NOR-Flash*.

The two main types of volatile random-access semiconductor memory are static random-access memory (SRAM) and dynamic random-access memory (DRAM).

Mining Rig Components, Power Supply

Dan's Pro Tip: "If your motherboard is not a mining board, but rather a regular PC board, you will need some 20+4 Dual Multiple PSU Power Supply Cable Splitter Adapter cables. See my YouTube videos for more information."

A **power supply unit (PSU)** converts mains AC to low-voltage regulated DC power for the internal components of a computer. Modern personal computers universally use switched-mode power supplies. Some power supplies have a manual switch for selecting input voltage, while others automatically adapt to the mains voltage.

Most modern desktop personal computer power supplies conform to the ATX specification, which includes form factor and voltage tolerances. While an ATX power supply is connected to the mains supply, it always provides a 5-volt standby (5VSB) power so that the standby functions on the computer and certain peripherals are powered. ATX power supplies are turned on and off by a signal from the motherboard. They also provide a signal to the motherboard to indicate when the DC voltages are in spec, so that the computer is able to safely power up and boot.

Mining Rig Power supply

Mining Rig Components, Power Supply, Modular Power Supplies

A modular power supply provides a detachable cable system, offering the ability to remove unused connections at the expense of a small amount of extra electrical resistance introduced by the additional connector.[35] This reduces clutter, removes the risk of dangling cables interfering with other components, and can improve case airflow. Many semi modular supplies have some permanent multi-wire cables with connectors at the ends, such as ATX motherboard and 8-pin EPS, though newer supplies marketed as "fully modular" allow even these to be disconnected.

The pin assignment of the detachable cables is only standardized on the output end and not on the end that is to be connected to the power supply. Thus, the cables of a modular power supply must only be used with this particular modular power supply model. Usage with another modular power supply, even if the cable prima facie appear compatible, might result in a wrong pin assignment and thus can lead to damage of connected components by supplying 12V to a 5V or 3.3V pin.[36]

Mining Rig Components, Power Supply, Modular Power Supplies, Ports

MB – mother board connection

CPU – connects to mother board to power the CPU

Perf – power to mother board Molex connector(s)

SATA – power to GPU PCI-E risers, also power to the SSD

VGA – power to the video cards

Mining Rig Components, Video Card

A **video card** (also called a **graphics card**, **display card**, **graphics adapter**, or **display adapter**) is an expansion card which generates a feed of output images to a display device (such as a computer monitor). Frequently, these are advertised as discrete or dedicated graphics, emphasizing the distinction between these and integrated graphics. At the core of both is the graphics processing unit (GPU), which is the main part that does the actual computations, but should not be confused with the video card as a whole, although "GPU" is often used as a metonymic shorthand to refer to video cards.

The integrated graphics processor on video cards can perform additional processing, removing this task from the central processor of the computer.[1] For example, Nvidia and AMD (previously ATI) produced cards that render the graphics pipelines OpenGL and DirectX on the hardware level.[2] In the later 2010s, there has also been a tendency to use the computing capabilities of the graphics processor to solve non-graphic tasks, which can be done through the use of OpenCL and CUDA. Video cards can also be used for AI training.[3][2]

Mining Rig Video Cards

Usually, the graphics card is made in the form of a printed

circuit board (expansion board) and inserted into an expansion slot, universal or specialized (AGP, PCI Express).[4] Some have been made using dedicated enclosures, which are connected to the computer via a docking station or a cable. These are known as eGPUs.

Mining Rig Components, Video Card, Power Demand

As the processing power of video cards has increased, so has their demand for electrical power. Current high-performance video cards tend to consume large amounts of power. For example, the thermal design power (TDP) for the GeForce Titan RTX is 280 watts.[10] When tested while gaming, the GeForce RTX 2080 Ti Founder's Edition averaged 300 watts of power consumption.[11] While CPU and power supply makers have recently moved toward higher efficiency, power demands of GPUs have continued to rise, so video cards may have the largest power consumption of any individual part in a computer.[12][13] Although power supplies are increasing their power too, the bottleneck is due to the PCI-Express connection, which is limited to supplying 75 watts.[14] Modern video cards with a power consumption of over 75 watts usually include a combination of six-pin (75 W) or eight-pin (150 W) sockets that connect directly to the power supply. Providing adequate cooling becomes a challenge in such computers. Computers with multiple video cards may require power supplies over 750 watts. Heat extraction becomes a major design consideration for computers with two or more high-end video cards.

Mining Rig Components, Video Card, Size

Video cards for desktop computers come in one of two size profiles, which can allow a graphics card to be added even to small-sized PCs. Some video cards are not of the usual size, and are thus categorized as being low profile.[15][16] Video card profiles are based on height only, with low-profile cards taking up less than the height of a PCIe slot, some can be as low as "half-height".[*citation needed*] Length and thickness can vary greatly, with high-end cards usually occupying two or three expansion slots, and with dual-GPU cards -such as the Nvidia GeForce GTX 690- generally exceeding 250 mm (10 in) in length.[17] Generally, most users will prefer a lower profile card if the intention is to fit multiple cards or they run into clearance issues with other motherboard components like the DIMM or PCIE slots. This can be fixed with a larger case that comes in sizes like a mid-tower and full tower. Full towers can usually fit larger motherboards in sizes like ATX and micro ATX. The larger the case, the larger the motherboard, the larger the graphics card or multiple other components that will acquire case real-estate.

Mining Rig Components, Video Card, Parts

A modern video card consists of a printed circuit board on which the components are mounted.

Mining Rig Components, Video Card, Parts, Graphics Processing Unit

A **graphics processing unit (GPU)** is a specialized electronic circuit designed to rapidly manipulate and alter memory to accelerate the building of images in a frame buffer intended for output to a display. Because of the large degree of programmable computational complexity for such a task, a modern video card is also a computer unto itself.

Mining Rig Components, Video Card, Parts, Heat Sink

A heat sink is mounted on most modern graphics cards. A heat sink spreads out the heat produced by the graphics processing unit evenly throughout the heat sink and unit itself. The heat sink commonly has a fan mounted as well to cool the heat sink and the graphics processing unit. Not all cards have heat sinks, for example, some cards are liquid-cooled and instead have a water block; additionally, cards from the 1980s and early 1990s did not produce much heat, and did not require heatsinks. Most modern graphics cards need a proper thermal solution. This can be the liquid solution or heatsinks with an additional connected heat pipe usually made of copper for the best thermal transfer. The correct case; either Mid-tower or Full-tower or some other derivative, has to be properly configured for thermal management. This can be ample space with a proper push-pull or opposite configuration as well as liquid with a radiator either in lieu or with a fan setup.

Mining Rig Components, Video Card, Parts, Video BIOS

The video BIOS or firmware contains a minimal program for the initial set up and control of the video card. It may contain information on the memory timing, operating speeds and voltages of the graphics processor, RAM, and other details which can sometimes be changed.

The modern Video BIOS does not support all the functions of the video card, being only sufficient to identify and initialize the card to display one of a few frame buffer or text display modes. It does not support YUV to RGB translation, video scaling, pixel copying, compositing or any of the multitude of other 2D and 3D features of the video card.

Mining Rig Components, Video Card, Parts, Video Memory

The memory capacity of most modern video cards ranges from 2 GB to 24 GB.[46] But with up to 32 GB as of the last 2010s, the applications for graphics use is becoming more powerful and widespread. Since video memory needs to be accessed by the GPU and the display circuitry, it often uses special high-speed or multi-port memory, such as VRAM, WRAM, SGRAM, etc. Around 2003, the video memory was typically based on DDR technology. During and after that year, manufacturers moved towards DDR2, GDDR3, GDDR4, GDDR5, GDDR5X, and GDDR6. The effective memory clock rate in modern cards is generally between 2 GHz to 15 GHz.

Mining Rig Components, Video Card, Advanced Micro Devices

Advanced Micro Devices, Inc. (AMD) is an American multinational semiconductor company based in Santa Clara, California, that develops computer processors and related technologies for business and consumer markets. While it initially manufactured its own processors, the company later outsourced its manufacturing, a practice known as going fabless, after GlobalFoundries was spun off in 2009. AMD's main products include microprocessors, motherboard chipsets, embedded processors and graphics processors for servers, workstations, personal computers and embedded system applications.

Mining Rig Components, Video Card, Nvidia

Nvidia Corporation is an American multinational technology company incorporated in Delaware and based in Santa Clara, California.[2] It designs graphics processing units (GPUs) for the gaming and professional markets, as well as system on a chip units (SoCs) for the mobile computing and automotive market. Its primary GPU line, labeled "GeForce", is in direct competition with the GPUs of the "Radeon" brand by Advanced Micro Devices (AMD). Nvidia expanded its presence in the gaming industry with its handheld game consoles Shield Portable, Shield Tablet, and Shield Android TV and its cloud gaming service GeForce Now.

Mining Rig Components, PCI-E Riser

PCI Express riser is also called a GPU riser or a PCI-E extension. It converts the PCI Express X1 slot from the mother board to an external PCI Express X16 slot. The extended PCI-E X16 slot is mainly used on Ethereum GPU Mining rigs. PCI-E risers usually come with a 6 pin power cable and a USB 3.0 PCI-E signal sync cable. The SATA to 6 pin power cable provides power for the GPUs. The USB 3.0 extension cables ensure easy GPU placement in the mining rig frame.

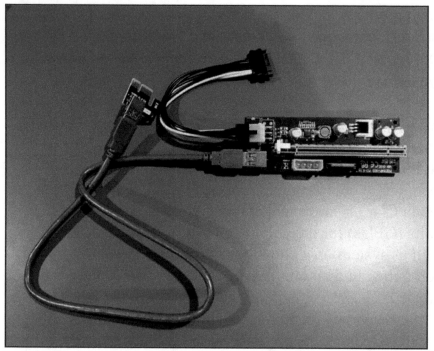

Mining Rig PCI-E Riser

Mining Rig Components, Solid-state Drive

A **solid-state drive** (**SSD**) is a solid-state storage device that uses integrated circuit assemblies to store data persistently, typically using flash memory, and functioning as secondary storage in the hierarchy of computer storage. It is also sometimes called a **solid-state device** or a **solid-state disk**,[1] even though SSDs lack the physical spinning disks and movable read–write heads used in hard disk drives (HDDs) and floppy disks.[2]

Compared with electromechanical drives, SSDs are typically more resistant to physical shock, run silently, and have quicker access time and lower latency.[3] SSDs store data in semiconductor cells. As of 2019, cells can contain between 1 and 4 bits of data. SSD storage devices vary in their properties according to the number of bits stored in each cell, with single-bit cells ("SLC") being generally the most reliable, durable, fast, and expensive type, compared with 2- and 3-bit cells ("MLC" and "TLC"), and finally quad-bit cells ("QLC") being used for consumer devices that do not require such extreme properties and are the cheapest of the four. In addition, 3D XPoint memory (sold by Intel under the Optane brand), stores data by changing the electrical resistance of cells instead of storing electrical charges in cells, and SSDs made from RAM can be used for high speed, when data persistence after power loss is not required, or may use battery power to retain data when its usual power source is unavailable.[4] Hybrid drives or solid-state hybrid drives (SSHDs), such as Apple's Fusion Drive, combine features of SSDs and HDDs in the same unit using both flash memory and a HDD in order to improve the performance of frequently-accessed data.[5][6] [7]

Mining Rig Solid-state Drive

SSDs based on NAND Flash will slowly leak charge over time if left for long periods without power. This causes worn-out drives (that have exceeded their endurance rating) to start losing data typically after one year (if stored at 30 °C) to two years (at 25 °C) in storage; for new drives it takes longer.[8] Therefore, SSDs are not suitable for archival storage. 3D XPoint is a possible exception to this rule; it is a relatively new technology with unknown long-term data-retention characteristics.

SSDs can use traditional HDD interfaces and form factors, or newer interfaces and form factors that exploit specific advantages of the flash memory in SSDs. Traditional interfaces (e.g. SATA and SAS) and standard HDD form factors allow such SSDs to be used as drop-in replacements for HDDs in computers and other devices. Newer form factors such as mSATA, M.2, U.2, NF1,[9][10] XFMEXPRESS[11] and EDSFF (formerly known as *Ruler SSD*)[12][13] and higher speed interfaces such as NVM Express (NVMe) over PCI Express can further increase performance over HDD performance.[4]

Mining Rig Components, Operating System

An **operating system (OS)** is system software that manages computer hardware, software resources, and provides common services for computer programs.

Time-sharing operating systems schedule tasks for efficient use of the system and may also include accounting software for cost allocation of processor time, mass storage, printing, and other resources.

For hardware functions such as input and output and memory allocation, the operating system acts as an intermediary between programs and the computer hardware, [1][2] although the application code is usually executed directly by the hardware and frequently makes system calls to an OS function or is interrupted by it. Operating systems are found on many devices that contain a computer – from cellular phones and video game consoles to web servers and supercomputers.

The dominant general-purpose[3] desktop operating system is Microsoft Windows with a market share of around

76.45%. macOS by Apple Inc. is in second place (17.72%), and the varieties of Linux are collectively in third place (1.73%).[4] In the mobile sector (including smartphones and tablets), Android's share is up to 72% in the year 2020. [5] According to third quarter 2016 data, Android's share on smartphones is dominant with 87.5 percent with also a growth rate of 10.3 percent per year, followed by Apple's iOS with 12.1 percent with per year decrease in market share of 5.2 percent, while other operating systems amount to just 0.3 percent.[6] Linux distributions are dominant in the server and supercomputing sectors. Other specialized classes of operating systems (special-purpose operating systems)[7][8]), such as embedded and real-time systems, exist for many applications. Security-focused operating systems also exist. Some operating systems have low system requirements (i.e. light-weight Linux distribution). Others may have higher system requirements.

Dan's Pro Tip: "I use Hive OS. Watch my YouTube videos to see why you will want to use Hive OS too."

Section 3
Tuning for Maximum Performance

Overclocking

Dan's Pro Tip: "This section is a must read; what you learn here will be combined with my specific YouTube videos on video card tuning."

In computing, **overclocking** is the practice of increasing the clock rate of a computer to exceed that certified by the manufacturer. Commonly, operating voltage is also increased to maintain a component's operational stability at accelerated speeds. Semiconductor devices operated at higher frequencies and voltages increase power consumption and heat.[1] An overclocked device may be unreliable or fail completely if the additional heat load is not removed or power delivery components cannot meet increased power demands. Many device warranties state that overclocking and/or over-specification voids any warranty, however there are an increasing number of manufacturers that will allow overclocking as long as performed (relatively) safely.

Overclocking, Overview

The purpose of overclocking is to increase the operating speed of a given component. Normally, on modern systems, the target of overclocking is increasing the performance of a major chip or subsystem, such as the main processor or graphics controller, but other components, such as system memory (RAM) or system buses (generally on the motherboard), are commonly involved. The trade-offs are an increase in power consumption (heat), fan noise (cooling), and shortened lifespan for the targeted components. Most components are designed with a margin of safety to deal with operating conditions outside of a manufacturer's control; examples are ambient temperature and fluctuations in operating voltage. Overclocking techniques in general aim to trade this safety margin by setting the device to run in the higher end of the margin, with the understanding that temperature and voltage must be more strictly monitored and controlled by the user. Examples are that operating temperature would need to be more strictly controlled with increased cooling, as the part will be less tolerant of increased temperatures at the higher speeds. Also base operating voltage may be increased to compensate for unexpected voltage drops and to strengthen signalling and timing signals, as low-voltage excursions are more likely to cause malfunctions at higher operating speeds.

While most modern devices are fairly tolerant of overclocking, all devices have finite limits. Generally for any given voltage most parts will have a maximum "stable" speed where they still operate correctly. Past this speed the device starts giving incorrect results, which can cause malfunctions and sporadic behavior in any system depending on it. While in a PC context the usual result is a system crash, more subtle errors can go undetected, which over a long enough time can give unpleasant surprises such as data corruption (incorrectly calculated results, or worse *writing to storage* incorrectly) or the system failing only during certain specific tasks (general usage such as internet browsing and word processing appear fine, but any application wanting advanced graphics crashes the system).

At this point an increase in operating voltage of a part may allow more headroom for further increases in clock speed, but the increased voltage can also significantly increase heat output, as well as shorten the lifespan further. At some point there will be a limit imposed by the ability to supply the device with sufficient power, the user's ability to cool the part, and the device's own maximum voltage tolerance before it achieves destructive failure. Overzealous use of voltage and/or inadequate cooling can rapidly degrade a device's performance to the point of failure, or in extreme cases outright destroy it.

The speed gained by overclocking depends largely upon the applications and workloads being run on the system, and what components are being overclocked by the user; benchmarks for different purposes are published.

Overclocking, Overview, Underclocking

Conversely, the primary goal of underclocking is to reduce power consumption and the resultant heat generation of a device, with the trade-offs being lower clock speeds and reductions in performance. Reducing the cooling requirements needed to keep hardware at a given operational temperature has knock-on benefits such as lowering the number and speed of fans to allow quieter operation, and in mobile devices increase the length of battery life per charge. Some manufacturers underclock components of battery-powered equipment to improve battery life, or implement systems that detect when a device is operating under battery power and reduce clock frequency Underclocking and undervolting would be attempted on a desktop system to have it operate silently (such as for a home entertainment center) while potentially offering higher performance than currently offered by low-voltage processor offerings. This would use a "standard-voltage" part and attempt to run with lower voltages (while attempting to keep the desktop speeds) to meet an acceptable performance/noise target for the build. This was also attractive as using a "standard voltage" processor in a "low voltage" application avoided paying the traditional price premium for an officially certified low voltage version. However again like overclocking there is no guarantee of success, and the builder's time researching given system/processor combinations and especially the time and tedium of performing many iterations of stability testing need to be considered. The usefulness of underclocking (again like overclocking) is determined by what processor offerings, prices, and availability are at the specific time of the build. Underclocking is also sometimes used when troubleshooting.

Overclocking, Overview, Enthusiast Culture

Overclocking has become more accessible with motherboard makers offering overclocking as a marketing feature on their mainstream product lines. However, the practice is embraced more by enthusiasts than professional users, as overclocking carries a risk of reduced reliability, accuracy and damage to data and equipment. Additionally, most manufacturer warranties and service agreements do not cover overclocked components nor any incidental damages caused by their use. While overclocking can still be an option for increasing personal computing capacity, and thus workflow productivity for professional users, the importance of stability testing components thoroughly *before* employing them into a production environment cannot be overstated.

Overclocking offers several draws for overclocking enthusiasts. Overclocking allows testing of components at speeds not currently offered by the manufacturer, or at speeds only officially offered on specialized, higher-priced versions of the product. A general trend in the computing industry is that new technologies tend to debut in the high-end market first, then later trickle down to the performance and mainstream market. If the high-end part only differs by an increased clock speed, an enthusiast can attempt to overclock a mainstream part to simulate the high-end offering. This can give insight on how over-the-horizon technologies will perform before they are officially available on the mainstream market, which can be especially helpful for other users considering if they should plan ahead to purchase or upgrade to the new feature when it is officially released.

Some hobbyists enjoy building, tuning, and "Hot-Rodding" their systems in competitive benchmarking competitions, competing with other like-minded users for high scores in standardized computer benchmark suites. Others will purchase a low-cost model of a component in a given product line, and attempt to overclock that part to match a more expensive model's stock performance. Another approach is overclocking older components to attempt to keep pace with increasing system requirements and extend the useful service life of the older part or at least delay a purchase of new hardware solely for performance reasons. Another rationale for overclocking older equipment is even if overclocking stresses equipment to the point of failure earlier, little is lost as it is already depreciated, and would have needed to be replaced in any case.[2]

Overclocking, Overview, Components

Technically any component that uses a timer (or clock) to synchronize its internal operations can be overclocked. Most efforts for computer components however focus on specific components, such as, processors (a.k.a. CPU), video cards, motherboard chipsets, and RAM. Most modern processors derive their effective operating speeds by multiplying a base clock (processor bus speed) by an internal multiplier within the processor (the CPU multiplier) to attain their final speed.

Computer processors generally are overclocked by manipulating the CPU multiplier if that option is available, but the processor and other components can also be overclocked by increasing the base speed of the bus clock. Some systems allow additional tuning of other clocks (such as a system clock) that influence the bus clock speed that, again is multiplied by the processor to allow for finer adjustments of the final processor speed.

Most OEM systems do not expose to the user the adjustments needed to change processor clock speed or voltage in the BIOS of the OEM's motherboard, which precludes overclocking (for warranty and support reasons). The same processor installed on a different motherboard offering adjustments will allow the user to change them.

Any given component will ultimately stop operating reliably past a certain clock speed. Components will generally show some sort of malfunctioning behavior or other indication of compromised stability that alerts the user that a given speed is not stable, but there is always a possibility that a component will permanently fail without warning, even if voltages are kept within some pre-determined safe values. The maximum speed is determined by overclocking to the point of first instability, then accepting the last stable slower setting. Components are only guaranteed to operate correctly up to their rated values; beyond that different samples may have different overclocking potential. The end-point of a given overclock is determined by parameters such as available CPU multipliers, bus dividers, voltages; the user's ability to manage thermal loads, cooling techniques; and several other factors of the individual devices themselves such as semiconductor clock and thermal tolerances, interaction with other components and the rest of the system.

Overclocking, Considerations

There are several things to be considered when overclocking. First is to ensure that the component is supplied with adequate power at a voltage sufficient to operate at the new clock rate. Supplying the power with improper settings or applying excessive voltage can permanently damage a component.

In a professional production environment, overclocking is only likely to be used where the increase in speed justifies the cost of the expert support required, the possibly reduced reliability, the consequent effect on maintenance contracts and warranties, and the higher power consumption. If faster speed is required it is often cheaper when all costs are considered to buy faster hardware.

Overclocking, Considerations, Cooling

All electronic circuits produce heat generated by the movement of electric current. As clock frequencies in digital circuits and voltage applied increase, the heat generated by components running at the higher performance levels also increases. The relationship between clock frequencies and thermal design power (TDP) are linear. However, there is a limit to the maximum frequency which is called a "wall". To overcome this issue, overclockers raise the chip voltage to increase the overclocking potential. Voltage increases power consumption and consequently heat generation significantly (proportionally to the square of the voltage in a linear circuit, for example); this requires more cooling to avoid damaging the hardware by overheating. In addition, some digital circuits slow down at high temperatures due to changes in MOSFET device characteristics. Conversely, the overclocker may decide to *decrease* the chip voltage while overclocking (a process known as undervolting), to reduce heat emissions while performance remains optimal.

Stock cooling systems are designed for the amount of power produced during non-overclocked use; overclocked circuits can require more cooling, such as by powerful fans, larger heat sinks, heat pipes and water cooling. Mass, shape, and material all influence the ability of a heatsink to dissipate heat. Efficient heatsinks are often made entirely of copper, which has high thermal conductivity, but is expensive.[3] Aluminium is more widely used; it has good thermal characteristics, though not as good as copper, and is significantly cheaper. Cheaper materials such as steel do not have good thermal characteristics. Heat pipes can be used to improve conductivity. Many heatsinks combine two or more materials to achieve a balance between performance and cost.[3]

Water cooling carries waste heat to a radiator. Thermoelectric cooling devices which actually refrigerate using the Peltier effect can help with high thermal design power (TDP) processors made by Intel and AMD in the early twenty-first century. Thermoelectric cooling devices create temperature differences between two plates by running an electric current through the plates. This method of cooling is highly effective, but itself generates significant heat elsewhere which must be carried away, often by a convection-based heatsink or a water cooling system.

Other cooling methods are forced convection and phase

transition cooling which is used in refrigerators and can be adapted for computer use. Liquid nitrogen, liquid helium, and dry ice are used as coolants in extreme cases,[4] such as record-setting attempts or one-off experiments rather than cooling an everyday system. In June 2006, IBM and Georgia Institute of Technology jointly announced a new record in silicon-based chip clock rate (the rate a transistor can be switched at, not the CPU clock rate[5]) above 500 GHz, which was done by cooling the chip to 4.5 K (−268.6 °C; −451.6 °F) using liquid helium.[6] CPU Frequency World Record is 8.794 GHz as of November 2012.[7] These extreme methods are generally impractical in the long term, as they require refilling reservoirs of vaporizing coolant, and condensation can form on chilled components.[4] Moreover, silicon-based junction gate field-effect transistors (JFET) will degrade below temperatures of roughly 100 K (−173 °C; −280 °F) and eventually cease to function or "freeze out" at 40 K (−233 °C; −388 °F) since the silicon ceases to be semiconducting,[8] so using extremely cold coolants may cause devices to fail.

Submersion cooling, used by the Cray-2 supercomputer, involves sinking a part of computer system directly into a chilled liquid that is thermally conductive but has low electrical conductivity. The advantage of this technique is that no condensation can form on components.[9] A good submersion liquid is Fluorinert made by 3M, which is expensive. Another option is mineral oil, but impurities such as those in water might cause it to conduct electricity. [9]

Amateur overclocking enthusiasts have used a mixture of dry ice and a solvent with a low freezing point, such as acetone or isopropyl alcohol.[10] This cooling bath, often used in laboratories, achieves a temperature of −78 °C.[11] However, this practice is discouraged due to its safety risks; the solvents are flammable and volatile, and dry ice can cause frostbite (through contact with exposed skin) and suffocation (due to the large volume of carbon dioxide generated when it sublimes).

Overclocking, Considerations, Stability and Functional Correctness

As an overclocked component operates outside of the manufacturer's recommended operating conditions, it may function incorrectly, leading to system instability. Another risk is silent data corruption by undetected errors. Such failures might never be correctly diagnosed and may instead be incorrectly attributed to software bugs in applications, device drivers, or the operating system. Overclocked use may permanently damage components enough to cause them to misbehave (even under normal operating conditions) without becoming totally unusable.

A large-scale 2011 field study of hardware faults causing a system crash for consumer PCs and laptops showed a four to 20 times increase (depending on CPU manufacturer) in system crashes due to CPU failure for overclocked computers over an eight-month period.[12]

In general, overclockers claim that testing can ensure that an overclocked system is stable and functioning correctly. Although software tools are available for testing hardware stability, it is generally impossible for any private individual to thoroughly test the functionality of a processor.[13]

Achieving good fault coverage requires immense engineering effort; even with all of the resources dedicated to validation by manufacturers, faulty components and even design faults are not always detected.

A particular "stress test" can verify only the functionality of the specific instruction sequence used in combination with the data and may not detect faults in those operations. For example, an arithmetic operation may produce the correct result but incorrect flags; if the flags are not checked, the error will go undetected.

To further complicate matters, in process technologies such as silicon on insulator (SOI), devices display hysteresis—a circuit's performance is affected by the events of the past, so without carefully targeted tests it is possible for a particular sequence of state changes to work at overclocked rates in one situation but not another even if the voltage and temperature are the same. Often, an overclocked system which passes stress tests experiences instabilities in other programs.[14]

In overclocking circles, "stress tests" or "torture tests" are used to check for correct operation of a component. These workloads are selected as they put a very high load on the component of interest (e.g. a graphically intensive application for testing video cards, or different math-intensive applications for testing general CPUs). Popular stress tests include Prime95, Everest, Superpi, OCCT, AIDA64, Linpack (via the LinX and IntelBurnTest GUIs), SiSoftware Sandra, BOINC, Intel Thermal Analysis Tool and Memtest86. The hope is that any functional-correctness issues with the overclocked component will show up during these tests, and if no errors are detected during the test, the component is then deemed "stable". Since fault coverage is important in stability testing, the tests are often run for long periods of time, hours or even days. An overclocked computer is sometimes described using the number of hours and the stability program used, such as "prime 12 hours stable".

Overclocking, Considerations, Factors Allowing Overclocking

Overclockability arises in part due to the economics of the manufacturing processes of CPUs and other components. In many cases components are manufactured by the same process, and tested after manufacture to determine their actual maximum ratings. Components are then marked with a rating chosen by the market needs of the semiconductor manufacturer. If manufacturing yield is high, more higher-rated components than required may be produced, and the manufacturer may mark and sell higher-performing components as lower-rated for marketing reasons. In some cases, the true maximum rating of the component may exceed even the highest rated component sold. Many devices sold with a lower rating may behave in all ways as higher-rated ones, while in the worst case operation at the higher rating may be more problematical.

Notably, higher clocks must always mean greater waste heat generation, as semiconductors set to high must dump to ground more often. In some cases, this means that the chief drawback of the overclocked part is far more heat dissipated than the maximums published by the manufacturer. Pentium architect Bob Colwell calls overclocking an "uncontrolled experiment in better-than-worst-case system operation".[15]

Overclocking, Considerations, Measuring Effects of Overclocking

Benchmarks are used to evaluate performance, and they can become a kind of "sport" in which users compete for the highest scores. As discussed above, stability and functional correctness may be compromised when overclocking, and meaningful benchmark results depend on the correct execution of the benchmark. Because of this, benchmark scores may be qualified with stability and correctness notes (e.g. an overclocker may report a score, noting that the benchmark only runs to completion 1 in 5 times, or that signs of incorrect execution such as display corruption are visible while running the benchmark). A widely used test of stability is Prime95, which has built-in error checking that fails if the computer is unstable.

Using only the benchmark scores, it may be difficult to judge the difference overclocking makes to the overall performance of a computer. For example, some benchmarks test only one aspect of the system, such as memory bandwidth, without taking into consideration how higher clock rates in this aspect will improve the system performance as a whole. Apart from demanding applications such as video encoding, high-demand databases and scientific computing, memory bandwidth is typically not a bottleneck, so a great increase in memory bandwidth may be unnoticeable to a user depending on the applications used. Other benchmarks, such as 3DMark, attempt to replicate game conditions.

Overclocking, Manufacturer and Vendor Overclocking

Commercial system builders or component resellers sometimes overclock to sell items at higher profit margins. The seller makes more money by overclocking lower-priced components which are found to operate correctly and selling equipment at prices appropriate for higher-rated components. While the equipment will normally operate correctly, this practice may be considered fraudulent if the buyer is unaware of it.

Overclocking is sometimes offered as a legitimate service or feature for consumers, in which a manufacturer or retailer tests the overclocking capability of processors, memory, video cards, and other hardware products. Several video card manufactures now offer factory-overclocked versions of their graphics accelerators, complete with a warranty, usually at a price intermediate between that of the standard product and a non-overclocked product of higher performance.

It is speculated that manufacturers implement overclocking prevention mechanisms such as CPU multiplier locking to prevent users from buying lower-priced items and overclocking them. These measures are sometimes marketed as a consumer protection benefit, but are often criticized by buyers.

Many motherboards are sold, and advertised, with extensive facilities for overclocking implemented in hardware and controlled by BIOS settings.[16]

Overclocking, Advantages

- Higher **performance** in games, en-/decoding, video editing and system tasks at no additional direct monetary expense, but with increased electrical consumption and thermal output.
- System **optimization**: Some systems have "bottlenecks", where small overclocking of one component can help realize the full potential of another component to a greater percentage than when just the limiting hardware itself is overclocked. For instance: many motherboards with AMD Athlon 64 processors limit the clock rate of four units of RAM to 333 MHz. However, the memory performance is computed by dividing the processor clock rate (which is a base number times a CPU multiplier, for instance 1.8 GHz is most likely 9×200 MHz) by a fixed integer such that, at a stock clock rate, the RAM would run at a clock rate near 333 MHz. Manipulating elements of how the processor clock rate is set (usually adjusting the multiplier), it is often possible to overclock the processor a small amount, around 5-10%, and gain a small increase in RAM clock rate and/or reduction in RAM latency timings.
- It can be **cheaper** to purchase a lower performance component and overclock it to the clock rate of a more expensive component.
- Extending life on older equipment (through underclocking/undervolting).

Overclocking, Disadvantages, General

- Higher clock rates and voltages increase **power consumption**, also increasing **electricity cost** and **heat production**. The additional heat increases the ambient air temperature within the system case, which may affect other components. The hot air blown out of the case heats the room it's in.

- Fan **noise**: High-performance fans running at maximum speed used for the required degree of cooling of an overclocked machine can be noisy, some producing 50 dB or more of noise. When maximum cooling is not required, in any equipment, fan speeds can be reduced below the maximum: fan noise has been found to be roughly proportional to the fifth power of fan speed; halving speed reduces noise by about 15 dB.[17] Fan noise can be reduced by design improvements, e.g. with aerodynamically optimized blades for smoother airflow, reducing noise to around 20 dB at approximately 1 metre[*citation needed*] or larger fans rotating more slowly, which produce less noise than smaller, faster fans with the same airflow. Acoustical insulation inside the case e.g. acoustic foam can reduce noise. Additional cooling methods which do not use fans can be used, such as liquid and phase-change cooling.

- An overclocked computer may become **unreliable**. For example: Microsoft Windows may appear to work with no problems, but when it is re-installed or upgraded, error messages may be received such as a "file copy error" during Windows Setup.[18]

Microsoft says this of errors in upgrading to Windows XP: "Your computer [may be] over-clocked." Because installing Windows is very memory-intensive, decoding errors may occur when files are extracted from the Windows XP CD-ROM.

- The **lifespan** of semiconductor components may be reduced by increased voltages and heat.
- Warranties may be voided by overclocking.

Overclocking, Disadvantages, Risks of Overclocking

- Increasing the operation frequency of a component will usually increase its thermal output in a linear fashion, while an increase in voltage usually causes thermal power to increase quadratically.[19] Excessive voltages or improper cooling may cause chip temperatures to rise to dangerous levels, causing the chip to be damaged or destroyed.
- Exotic cooling methods used to facilitate overclocking such as water cooling are more likely to cause damage if they malfunction. Sub-ambient cooling methods such as phase-change cooling or liquid nitrogen will cause water condensation, which will cause electrical damage unless controlled; some methods include using kneaded erasers or shop towels to catch the condensation.

Overclocking, Disadvantages, Limitations

Overclocking components can only be of noticeable benefit if the component is on the critical path for a process, if it is a bottleneck. If disk access or the speed of an Internet connection limit the speed of a process, a 20% increase in processor speed is unlikely to be noticed, however there are some scenarios where increasing the clock speed of a processor actually allows an SSD to be read and written to faster. Overclocking a CPU will not noticeably benefit a game when a graphics card's performance is the "bottleneck" of the game.

Overclocking, Disadvantages, Graphics Cards

Graphics cards can also be overclocked. There are utilities to achieve this, such as EVGA's Precision, RivaTuner, AMD Overdrive (on AMD cards only), MSI Afterburner, Zotac Firestorm, and the PEG Link Mode on Asus motherboards. Overclocking a GPU will often yield a marked increase in performance in synthetic benchmarks, usually reflected in game performance.[20] It is sometimes possible to see that a graphics card is being pushed beyond its limits before any permanent damage is done by observing on-screen artifacts or unexpected system crashes. It is common to run into one of those problems when overclocking graphics cards; both symptoms at the same time usually means that the card is severely pushed beyond its heat, clock rate, and/or voltage limits, however if seen when not overclocked, they indicate a faulty card. After a reboot, video settings are reset to standard values stored in the graphics card firmware, and the maximum clock rate of that specific card is now deducted.

Some overclockers apply a potentiometer to the graphics card to manually adjust the voltage (which usually invalidates the warranty). This allows for finer adjustments, as overclocking software for graphics cards can only go so far. Excessive voltage increases may damage or destroy components on the graphics card or the entire graphics card itself (practically speaking).

Overclocking, Disadvantages, Graphics Cards, Alternatives

Flashing and unlocking can be used to improve the performance of a video card, without technically overclocking (but is much riskier than overclocking just through software).

Flashing refers to using the firmware of a different card with the same (or sometimes similar) core and compatible firmware, effectively making it a higher model card; it can be difficult, and may be irreversible. Sometimes standalone software to modify the firmware files can be found, e.g. NiBiTor (GeForce 6/7 series are well regarded in this aspect), without using firmware for a better model video card. For example, video cards with 3D accelerators (most, as of 2011) have two voltage and clock rate settings, one for 2D and one for 3D, but were designed to operate with *three* voltage stages, the third being somewhere between the aforementioned two, serving as a fallback when the card overheats or as a middle-stage when going from 2D to 3D operation mode. Therefore, it could be wise to set this middle-stage prior to "serious" overclocking, specifically because of this fallback ability; the card can drop down to this clock rate, reducing by a few (or sometimes a few dozen, depending on the setting) percent of its efficiency and cool down, without dropping out of 3D mode (and afterwards return to the desired high performance clock and voltage settings).

Some cards have abilities not directly connected with overclocking. For example, Nvidia's GeForce 6600GT (AGP flavor) has a temperature monitor used internally by the card, invisible to the user if standard firmware is used. Modifying the firmware can display a 'Temperature' tab.

Unlocking refers to enabling extra pipelines or pixel shaders. The 6800LE, the 6800GS and 6800 (AGP models only) were some of the first cards to benefit from unlocking. While these models have either 8 or 12 pipes enabled, they share the same 16x6 GPU core as a 6800GT or Ultra, but pipelines and shaders beyond those specified are disabled; the GPU may be fully functional, or may have been found to have faults which do not affect operation at the lower specification. GPUs found to be fully functional can be unlocked successfully, although it is not possible to be sure that there are undiscovered faults; in the worst case the card may become permanently unusable.

Section 4
Power / Electricity

Dan's Pro Tip: "This is practically the most important section of the book. Knowing as much as you can about electricity will help you properly and safely set up your mining rigs. If you skip reading this section now, I guarantee you will come back and read it later when you start popping circuit breakers (and you will pop circuit breakers!)"

Mains Electricity

Mains electricity (Commonwealth English), also known by the American English terms **utility power, power grid, domestic power**, and **wall power**, or in some parts of Canada as **hydro**, is a general-purpose alternating-current (AC) electric power supply. It is the form of electrical power that is delivered to homes and businesses through electrical infrastructure in many parts of the world. People use this electricity to power everyday items—such as domestic appliances, televisions and lamps—by plugging them into a wall outlet.

The two principal properties of the electric power supply, voltage and frequency, differ between regions. A voltage of (nominally) 230 V and a frequency of 50 Hz is used in Europe, most of Africa, most of Asia, Australia, and much of South America. In North America, the most common combination is 120 V and a frequency of 60 Hz. Other voltages exist, and some countries may have, for example, 230 V at 60 Hz. This is a concern to travellers, since portable appliances designed for one voltage and frequency combination may not operate with, or may even be destroyed by another. The use of different and incompatible plugs and sockets in different regions and countries provides some protection from accidental use of appliances with incompatible voltage and frequency requirements.

Mains Electricity, Terminology

In the US, mains electric power is referred to by several names including "utility power", "household power", "household electricity", "house current", "powerline", "domestic power", "wall power", "line power", "AC power", "city power", "street power".

In the UK, mains electric power is generally referred to as "the mains". More than half of power in Canada is hydroelectricity, and mains electricity is often referred to there as "hydro". This is also reflected in names of current and historical electricity monopolies such as Hydro-Québec, BC Hydro, Manitoba Hydro, Newfoundland and Labrador Hydro, and Hydro One.

Mains Electricity, Power Systems

Worldwide, many different mains power systems are found for the operation of household and light commercial electrical appliances and lighting. The different systems are primarily characterized by their

- Voltage
- Frequency
- Plugs and sockets (receptacles or outlets)
- Earthing system (grounding)
- Protection against overcurrent damage (e.g., due to short circuit), electric shock, and fire hazards
- Parameter tolerances.

All these parameters vary among regions. The voltages are generally in the range 100–240 V (always expressed as root-mean-square voltage). The two commonly used frequencies are 50 Hz and 60 Hz. Single-phase or three-phase power is most commonly used today, although two-phase systems were used early in the 20th century. Foreign enclaves, such as large industrial plants or overseas military bases, may have a different standard voltage or frequency from the surrounding areas. Some city areas may use standards different from that of the surrounding countryside (e.g. in Libya). Regions in an effective state of anarchy may have no central electrical authority, with electric power provided by incompatible private sources.

Many other combinations of voltage and utility frequency were formerly used, with frequencies between 25 Hz and 133 Hz and voltages from 100 V to 250 V. Direct current (DC) has been almost completely displaced by alternating current (AC) in public power systems, but DC was used especially in some city areas to the end of the 20th century. The modern combinations of 230 V/50 Hz and 120 V/60 Hz, listed in IEC 60038, did not apply in the first few decades of the 20th century and are still not universal.

Industrial plants with three-phase power will have different, higher voltages installed for large equipment (and different sockets and plugs), but the common voltages listed here would still be found for lighting and portable equipment.

Mains Electricity, Building Wiring

In many countries, household power is single-phase electric power, with two or three wired contacts at each outlet. Neutral and line wires carry current and are defined as live parts.[4][5]

- The **line wire** (in IEC terms 'line conductor'[6]) also known as **phase**, **hot** or **active** contact (and commonly, but technically incorrectly, as *live*), carries alternating current between the power grid and the household.
- The **neutral wire** (IEC: neutral conductor [7]) completes the electrical circuit—remaining at a voltage in proximity to 0 V—by also carrying alternating current between the power grid and the household. The neutral is connected to the ground (Earth), and therefore has nearly the same electrical potential as the earth. This prevents the power circuits from increasing beyond earth voltage, such as when they are struck by lightning or become otherwise charged.
- The **earth wire**, **ground** or, in IEC terms, Protective Earth[8] (PE) connects the chassis of equipment to earth ground as a protection against faults (electric shock), such as if the insulation on a "hot" wire becomes damaged and the bare wire comes into

contact with the metal chassis or case of the equipment.

Further information: Ground and neutral

- Mixed 230 V/415 V three-phase (common in northern and central Europe) or 230 V single-phase based household wiring.

In northern and central Europe, residential electrical supply is commonly 400 V three-phase electric power, which gives 230 V between any single phase and neutral; house wiring may be a mix of three-phase and single-phase circuits, but three-phase residential use is rare in the UK. High-power appliances such as kitchen stoves, water heaters and maybe household power heavy tools like log splitters may be supplied from the 400 V three-phase power supply.

Various earthing systems are used to ensure that the ground and neutral wires have zero voltage with respect to earth, to prevent shocks when touching grounded electrical equipment. In some installations, there may be two line conductors which carry alternating currents in a single-phase three-wire. Small portable electrical equipment is connected to the power supply through flexible cables (these exist with either two or three insulated conductors) terminated in a plug, which is inserted into a fixed receptacle (socket). Larger household electrical equipment and industrial equipment may be permanently wired to the fixed wiring of the building. For example, in North American homes a window-mounted self-contained air conditioner unit would be connected to a wall plug, whereas the central air conditioning for a whole home would be permanently wired. Larger plug and socket combinations are used for industrial equipment carrying larger currents, higher voltages, or three phase electric power. These are often constructed with tougher plastics and possess inherent weather-resistant properties needed in some applications.

Circuit breakers and fuses are used to detect short circuits between the line and neutral or ground wires or the drawing of more current than the wires are rated to handle (overload protection) to prevent overheating and possible fire. These protective devices are usually mounted in a central panel— most commonly a distribution board or consumer unit—in a building, but some wiring systems also provide a protection device at the socket or within the plug. Residual-current devices, also known as ground-fault circuit interrupters and appliance leakage current interrupters, are used to detect *ground faults*—flow of current in other than the neutral and line wires (like the ground wire or a person). When a ground fault is detected, the device quickly cuts off the circuit.

Mains Electricity, Voltage Levels

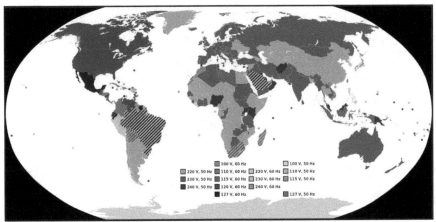

World Map of Mains Voltages and Frequencies, simplified

to country level. Use the web address below to see more detail.

https://en.wikipedia.org/wiki/Mains_electricity#/media/File: World_Map_of_Mains_Voltages_and_Frequencies,_Detaile d.svg

Most of the world population (Europe, Africa, Asia, Australia, New Zealand) and much of South America use a supply that is within 6% of 230 V. In the UK and Australia[9] the nominal supply voltage is 230 V +10%/ −6% to accommodate the fact that most transformers are in fact still set to 240 V. The 230 V standard has become widespread so that 230 V equipment can be used in most parts of the world with the aid of an adapter or a change to the equipment's plug to the standard for the specific country. The United States and Canada use a supply voltage of 120 volts ± 6%. Japan, Taiwan, Saudi Arabia, North America, Central America and some parts of northern South America use a voltage between 100 V and 127 V. Brazil is unusual in having both 127 V and 220 V systems at 60 Hz and also permitting interchangeable plugs and sockets.[10] Saudi Arabia and Mexico have mixed voltage systems; in residential and light commercial buildings both countries use 127 volts, with 220 volts in commercial and industrial applications. The Saudi government approved plans in August 2010 to transition the country to a totally 230/400 volts system,[11] but Mexico has no plans to transition.

Mains Electricity, Voltage Levels, Measuring Voltage

A distinction should be made between the voltage at the

point of supply (nominal voltage at the point of interconnection between the electrical utility and the user) and the voltage rating of the equipment (utilization voltage). Typically the utilization voltage is 3% to 5% lower than the nominal system voltage; for example, a nominal 208 V supply system will be connected to motors with "200 V" on their nameplates. This allows for the voltage drop between equipment and supply.[*citation needed*] Voltages in this article are the nominal supply voltages and equipment used on these systems will carry slightly lower nameplate voltages. Power distribution system voltage is nearly sinusoidal in nature. Voltages are expressed as root mean square (RMS) voltage. Voltage tolerances are for steady-state operation. Momentary heavy loads, or switching operations in the power distribution network, may cause short-term deviations out of the tolerance band and storms and other unusual conditions may cause even larger transient variations. In general, power supplies derived from large networks with many sources are more stable than those supplied to an isolated community with perhaps only a single generator.

Mains Electricity, Voltage Levels, Choice of Voltage

The choice of supply voltage is due more to historical reasons than optimization of the electric power distribution system—once a voltage is in use and equipment using this voltage is widespread, changing voltage is a drastic and expensive measure. A 230 V distribution system will use less conductor material than a 120 V system to deliver a given amount of power because the current, and consequently the resistive loss, is lower. While large heating appliances can use smaller conductors at 230 V for the same output rating, few household appliances use anything like the full capacity of the outlet to which they are connected. Minimum wire size for hand-held or portable equipment is usually restricted by the mechanical strength of the conductors. Electrical appliances are used extensively in homes in both 230 V and 120 V system countries. National electrical codes prescribe wiring methods intended to minimize the risk of electric shock and fire.

Many areas, such as the US, which use (nominally) 120 V, make use of three-wire, split-phase 240 V systems to supply large appliances. In this system a 240 V supply has a centre-tapped neutral to give two 120 V supplies which can also supply 240 V to loads connected between the two line wires. Three-phase systems can be connected to give various combinations of voltage, suitable for use by different classes of equipment. Where both single-phase and three-phase loads are served by an electrical system, the system may be labelled with both voltages such as 120/208 or 230/400 V, to show the line-to-neutral voltage and the line-to-line voltage. Large loads are connected for the higher voltage. Other three-phase voltages, up to 830 volts, are occasionally used for special-purpose systems such as oil well pumps. Large industrial motors (say, more than 250 hp or 150 kW) may operate on medium voltage. On 60 Hz systems a standard for medium voltage equipment is 2,400/4,160 V (2,300/4,000 V in the US) whereas 3,300 V is the common standard for 50 Hz systems.

Mains Electricity, Voltage Levels, Standardization

Until 1987, mains voltage in large parts of Europe, including Germany, Austria and Switzerland, was 220 V while the UK used 240 V. Standard ISO IEC 60038:1983 defined the new standard European voltage to be 230 V.

From 1987 onwards, a step-wise shift towards 230 V was implemented. From 2009 on, the voltage is permitted to be 230 V.[12][13] No change in voltage was required by either the Central European or the UK system, as both 220 V and 240 V fall within the lower 230 V tolerance bands (230 V ±6%). Some areas of the UK still have 250 volts for legacy reasons, but these also fall within the 10% tolerance band of 230 volts. In practice, this allowed countries to have supplied the same voltage (220 or 240 V), at least until existing supply transformers are replaced. Equipment (with the exception of filament bulbs) used in these countries is designed to accept any voltage within the specified range. In the United States[14][15] and Canada,[16] national standards specify that the nominal voltage at the source should be 120 V and allow a range of 114 V to 126 V (RMS) (−5% to +5%). Historically 110 V, 115 V and 117 V have been used at different times and places in North America. Mains power is sometimes spoken of as 110 V; however, 120 V is the nominal voltage.

In 2000, Australia converted to 230 V as the nominal standard with a tolerance of +10%/−6%,[17] this superseding the old 240 V standard, AS2926-1987. As in the UK, 240 V is within the allowable limits and "240 volt" is a synonym for mains in Australian and British English. In

Japan, the electrical power supply to households is at 100 V. Eastern and northern parts of Honshū (including Tokyo) and Hokkaidō have a frequency of 50 Hz, whereas western Honshū (including Nagoya, Osaka, and Hiroshima), Shikoku, Kyūshū and Okinawa operate at 60 Hz. The boundary between the two regions contains four back-to-back high-voltage direct-current (HVDC) substations which interconnect the power between the two grid systems; these are Shin Shinano, Sakuma Dam, Minami-Fukumitsu, and the Higashi-Shimizu Frequency Converter. To accommodate the difference, frequency-sensitive appliances marketed in Japan can often be switched between the two frequencies.

Mains Electricity, History

The world's first public electricity supply was a water wheel driven system constructed in the small English town of Godalming in 1881. It was an alternating current (AC) system using a Siemens alternator supplying power for both street lights and consumers at two voltages, 250 V for arc lamps, and 40 V for incandescent lamps.[18]

The world's first large scale central plant—Thomas Edison's steam powered station at Holborn Viaduct in London—started operation in January 1882, providing direct current (DC) at 110 V.[19] The Holborn Viaduct station was used as a proof of concept for the construction of the much larger Pearl Street Station in Manhattan, the world's first permanent commercial central power plant. The Pearl Street Station also provided DC at 110 V, considered to be a "safe" voltage for consumers, beginning

September 4, 1882.[20]

AC systems started appearing in the US in the mid-1880s, using higher distribution voltage stepped down via transformers to the same 110 V customer utilization voltage that Edison used. In 1883 Edison patented a three–wire distribution system to allow DC generation plants to serve a wider radius of customers to save on copper costs. By connecting two groups of 110 V lamps in series more load could be served by the same size conductors run with 220 V between them; a neutral conductor carried any imbalance of current between the two sub-circuits. AC circuits adopted the same form during the war of the currents, allowing lamps to be run at around 110 V and major appliances to be connected to 220 V. Nominal voltages gradually crept upward to 112 V and 115 V, or even 117 V.[*citation needed*] After World War II the standard voltage in the U.S. became 117 V, but many areas lagged behind even into the 1960s. [*citation needed*] In 1967 the nominal voltage rose to 120 V, but conversion of appliances was slow.[*citation needed*] Today, virtually all American homes and businesses have access to 120 and 240 V at 60 Hz. Both voltages are available on the three wires (two "hot" legs of opposite phase and one "neutral" leg).

In 1899, the Berliner Elektrizitäts-Werke (BEW), a Berlin electrical utility, decided to greatly increase its distribution capacity by switching to 220 V nominal distribution, taking advantage of the higher voltage capability of newly developed metal filament lamps. The company was able to offset the cost of converting the customer's equipment by the resulting saving in distribution conductors cost. This became the model for electrical distribution in Germany and the rest of Europe and the 220 V system became common. North American practice remained with voltages near 110 V for lamps.[21]

In the first decade after the introduction of alternating current in the US (from the early 1880s to about 1893) a variety of different frequencies were used, with each electric provider setting their own, so that no single one prevailed. The most common frequency was 133⅓ Hz. [*citation needed*] The rotation speed of induction generators and motors, the efficiency of transformers, and flickering of carbon arc lamps all played a role in frequency setting. Around 1893 the Westinghouse Electric Company in the United States and AEG in Germany decided to standardize their generation equipment on 60 Hz and 50 Hz respectively, eventually leading to most of the world being supplied at one of these two frequencies. Today most 60 Hz systems deliver nominal 120/240 V, and most 50 Hz nominally 230 V. The significant exceptions are in Brazil, which has a synchronized 60 Hz grid with both 127 V and 220 V as standard voltages in different regions,[22] and Japan, which has two frequencies: 50 Hz for East Japan and 60 Hz for West Japan.

Mains Electricity, Voltage Regulation

To maintain the voltage at the customer's service within the acceptable range, electrical distribution utilities use regulating equipment at electrical substations or along the distribution line. At a substation, the step-down transformer will have an automatic on-load tap changer, allowing the ratio between transmission voltage and distribution voltage to be adjusted in steps. For long (several kilometres) rural distribution circuits, automatic voltage regulators may be mounted on poles of the distribution line. These are autotransformers, again, with on-load tap changers to adjust the ratio depending on the observed voltage changes. At each customer's service, the step-down transformer has up to five taps to allow some range of adjustment, usually ±5% of the nominal voltage. Since these taps are not automatically controlled, they are used only to adjust the long-term average voltage at the service and not to regulate the voltage seen by the utility customer.

Mains Electricity, Power Quality

The stability of the voltage and frequency supplied to customers varies among countries and regions. "Power quality" is a term describing the degree of deviation from the nominal supply voltage and frequency. Short-term surges and drop-outs affect sensitive electronic equipment such as computers and flat panel displays. Longer-term power outages, brown-outs and black outs and low reliability of supply generally increase costs to customers, who may have to invest in uninterruptible power supply or stand-by generator sets to provide power when the utility supply is unavailable or unusable. Erratic power supply may be a severe economic handicap to businesses and public services which rely on electrical machinery, illumination, climate control and computers. Even the best quality power system may have breakdowns or require servicing. As such, companies, governments and other organizations sometimes have backup generators at sensitive facilities, to ensure that power will be available even in the event of a power outage or black out.

Power quality can also be affected by distortions of the current or voltage waveform in the form of harmonics of the fundamental (supply) frequency, or non-harmonic (inter)modulation distortion such as that caused by RFI or EMI interference. In contrast, harmonic distortion is usually caused by conditions of the load or generator. In multi-phase power, phase shift distortions caused by imbalanced loads can occur.

Ohm's Law

Dan's Pro Tip: "Be sure to know this: Power in Watts (heat) = Voltage multiplied by the current (Amps) (P = V x I). Your mining rigs will be producing a lot of heat. While the below reads a bit different, it is the same concept."

Ohm's law states that the current through a conductor between two points is directly proportional to the voltage across the two points. Introducing the constant of proportionality, the resistance,[1] one arrives at the usual mathematical equation that describes this relationship:[2]

$$I = V / R$$

where I is the current through the conductor in units of amperes, V is the voltage measured *across* the conductor in units of volts, and R is the resistance of the conductor in units of ohms. More specifically, Ohm's law states that the R in this relation is constant, independent of the current.[3] Ohm's law is an empirical relation which accurately describes the conductivity of the vast majority of electrically conductive materials over many orders of magnitude of current. However some materials do not obey Ohm's law, these are called non-ohmic.

Ampere (Amps)

Dan's Pro Tip: "This explaination of Amps goes deep quick, don't sweat it. Just know this: your facility / house is limited in the number of Amps it is wired for. Also, just because a circuit breaker is rated for 15 Amps, it will likly pop with a load of 12 or more Amps (use the rule of 80%; at 80% load the breaker could trip/pop)."

The **ampere**,[4] often shortened to "amp",[5] is the base unit of electric current in the International System of Units (SI).[6][7] It is named after André-Marie Ampère (1775–1836), French mathematician and physicist, considered the father of electromagnetism.
The International System of Units defines the ampere in terms of other base units by measuring the electromagnetic force between electrical conductors carrying electric current. The earlier CGS system had two different

definitions of current, one essentially the same as the SI's and the other using electric charge as the base unit, with the unit of charge defined by measuring the force between two charged metal plates. The ampere was then defined as one coulomb of charge per second.[8] In SI, the unit of charge, the coulomb, is defined as the charge carried by one ampere during one second.

AC Power Plugs and Sockets

AC power plugs and sockets connect electric equipment to the alternating current (AC) power supply in buildings and at other sites. Electrical plugs and sockets differ from one another in voltage and current rating, shape, size, and connector type. Different standard systems of plugs and sockets are used around the world.

Plugs and sockets for portable appliances became available in the 1880s, to replace connections to light sockets with wall-mounted outlets. A proliferation of types developed for both convenience and protection from electrical injury. Today there are about 20 types in common use around the world, and many obsolete socket types are found in older buildings. Coordination of technical standards has allowed some types of plug to be used across large regions to facilitate trade in electrical appliances, and for the convenience of travellers and consumers of imported electrical goods.

Some multi-standard sockets allow use of several types of plug; improvised or unapproved adaptors between incompatible sockets and plugs may not provide the full safety and performance of an approved socket-plug combination.

AC Power Plugs and Sockets, Concepts and Terminology

A plug is the movable connector attached to an electrically operated device, and the socket is fixed on equipment or a building structure and connected to an energised electrical circuit. The plug is a *male* connector with protruding pins that match the openings and *female* contacts in a socket. Some plugs have female contacts that are used only for an earth ground connection. Some plugs have built-in fuses for safety.

To reduce the risk of electric shock, plug and socket systems have safety features in addition to the recessed contacts of the energised socket. These may include plugs with insulated sleeves, recessed sockets, or automatic shutters to block socket apertures when a plug is removed.

A socket may be surrounded by a decorative or protective cover[1] which may be integral with the socket.

Single-phase sockets have two current-carrying connections to the power supply circuit, and may also have a third pin for a safety connection to earth ground. Depending on the supply system, one or both current-carrying connections may have significant voltage to earth ground.

AC Power Plugs and Sockets, Voltage Rating of Plugs and Power Cords

Plugs and power cords have a rated voltage and current assigned to them by the manufacturer. Using a plug or power cord that is inappropriate for the load may be a safety hazard. For example, high-current equipment can cause a fire when plugged into an extension cord with a current rating lower than necessary. Sometimes the cords used to plug in dual voltage 120 V / 240 V equipment are rated only for 125 V, so care must be taken by miners to use only cords with an appropriate voltage rating.

AC Power Plugs and Sockets, Appliance Connections and Extensions

So that manufacturers need not build many similar appliances differing only in the type of plug fitted, a common strategy is to provide an IEC 60320 inlet on the appliance and a detachable power cord (mains flex lead) and appropriate plug. The appliance need only to be tested to the power inlet. Some appliances have a switch for selection of voltage.

Extension cords (extension leads) are used for temporary connections when a socket is not within convenient reach of an appliance's power lead. A power strip with multiple sockets may also have a switch, surge voltage protection, or over-current protection.

Power Cord

Dan's Pro Tip: "ALWAYS visually inspect your power cords before their first use, they will indicate what Voltage and how many Amps they are rated for."

North American power cord with IEC 60320 C13 appliance connector and NEMA 5-15 wall plug.

A **power cord**, **line cord**, or **mains cable** is an electrical cable that temporarily connects an appliance to the mains electricity supply via a wall socket or extension cord. The terms are generally used for cables using a power plug to connect to a single-phase alternating current power source at the local line voltage (generally 100 to 240 volts, depending on the location). The terms **power cable**, **mains lead**, **flex** or **kettle lead** are also used. A **lamp cord** (also known as a **zip cord**) is a light-weight, ungrounded, single-insulated two-wire cord used for small loads such as a table or floor lamp.

A **cord set** includes connectors molded to the cord at each end (see Appliance coupler). Cord sets are detachable from both the power supply and the electrical equipment, and consist of a flexible cord with electrical connectors at either end, one male, and one female. One end of the cord set is attached to a molded electrical plug; the other is typically a molded electrical receptacle to prevent the possibility of having an exposed live prong or pin which would cause electric shock. The female connector attaches to the piece of equipment or appliance while the male plug connects to the electrical receptacle or outlet.

Power Cord, Features

Power cables may be either fixed or detachable from the appliance.[1] In the case of detachable leads, the appliance end of the power cord has a female connector to link it to the appliance, to avoid the dangers from having a live protruding pin. Cords may also have twist-locking features, or other attachments to prevent accidental disconnection at one or both ends. A cord set may include accessories such as fuses for overcurrent protection, a pilot lamp to indicate voltage is present, or a leakage current detector. Power cords for sensitive instruments, or audio/video equipment may also include a shield over the power conductors to minimize electromagnetic interference.

A power cord or appliance coupler may have a retaining clamp, a mechanical device that prevents it from inadvertently being pulled or shaken loose. Typical application areas with stricter safety requirements include medical technology, stage and lighting technology, and computing equipment. For specialty equipment such as construction machinery, sound and lighting equipment, emergency medical defibrillators and electrical power tools, used in locations without a convenient power source, extension cords are used to carry the electric current up to hundreds of feet away from an outlet.

In North America, the National Electrical Manufacturers Association develops standards for electrical plugs and receptacles and cables.[2]

International power cords and plug adapters are used in conjunction with electrical appliances in countries different from those in which they were designed to operate. Besides a cord with one end compatible to receptacles or a device from one country and the other end compatible with receptacles or devices from another country, a voltage converter is usually necessary, as well, to protect travelers' electronic devices, such as laptops, from the differing voltages between the United States and places like Europe or Africa.

North American lamp cords have two single-insulated conductors designed for low-current applications. The insulator covering one of the conductors is ribbed (parallel to wire) for the entire length of the cord, while the other conductor's insulator is smooth. The smooth one is hot and the ribbed one is neutral.[3]

Power Cord, Connectors

IEC 60320 power cables come in normal and high-temperature variants, as well as various rated currents. The connectors have slightly different shapes to ensure that it is not possible to substitute a cable with a lower temperature or current rating, but that it *is* possible to use an overrated cable. Cords also have different types of exterior jackets available to accommodate environmental variables such as moisture, temperature, oils, sunlight, flexibility, and heavy wear. For example, a heating appliance may come with a cord designed to withstand accidental contact with heated surfaces.

Worldwide, more than a dozen different types of AC power plugs and sockets are used for fixed building wiring. Products sold in many different markets can use a standardized IEC 60320 connector and then use a detachable power cord to match the local electrical outlets. This simplifies safety approvals, factory testing, and production since the power cord is a low-cost item available as a commodity. Since the same types of appliance-side connectors are used with both 110 V and 230 V power cables, the user must ensure the connected equipment will operate with the available voltage. Some devices have a slide-switch to adapt to different voltages, or wide-ranging power supplies.

Power Cord, Standards

National electrical codes may apply to power cords and related items. For example, in the United States, power cords must meet UL Standards 62[4] and 817.[5]

Power Cord, Power Supplies

Cord sets must be distinguished from AC adapters, where the connector also contains a transformer, and possibly rectifiers, filters and regulators. Unwary substitution of a standard mains-voltage connector for the power supply would result in application of full line voltage to the connected device, resulting in its destruction and possible fire or personal injury.

Power Strip

A **power strip** (also known as an **extension block, extension box, power board, power bar, plug board, pivot plug, trailing gang, trailing socket, plug bar, trailer lead, multi-socket, multi-box, socket board, super plug, multiple socket, multiple outlet, polysocket** and by many other variations) is a block of electrical sockets that attaches to the end of a flexible cable (typically with a mains plug on the other end), allowing multiple electrical devices to be powered from a single electrical socket. Power strips are often used when many electrical devices are in proximity, such as for audio, video, computer systems, appliances, power tools, and lighting. Power strips often include a circuit breaker to interrupt the electric current in case of an overload or a short circuit. Some power strips provide protection against electrical power surges. Typical housing styles include strip, rack-mount, under-monitor and direct plug-in.[1]

Power Strip, Control

Some power strips include a master switch to turn all devices on and off. This can be used with simple devices, such as lights, but not with most computers, which must use shutdown commands from the software. Computers may have open files, which may be damaged if the power is simply turned off.

Some power strips have individually switched outlets.

"Master/slave" strips can detect one "master" device being turned off (such as the PC itself in a computer setup, or a TV in a home theatre) and turn everything else on or off accordingly.

Remote control strips are used in data centers, to allow computer systems or other devices to be remotely restarted, often over the Internet (although this leaves them vulnerable to outside attacks).[*citation needed*]

Power Strip, Indication

Many power strips have a neon or LED indicator light or one per output socket to show when power is on. Better-quality surge-protected strips have additional lights to indicate the status of the surge protection system, however these are not always reliable as an indicator.[2]

Power Strip, Energy-saving Features and Standby Power

Some power strips have energy-saving features, which switch off the strip if appliances go into standby mode. Using a sensor circuit, they detect if the level of power through the socket is in standby mode (less than 30 watts), and if so they will turn off that socket.[3][4] This reduces the consumption of standby power used by computer peripherals and other equipment when not in use, saving money and energy [5] Some more-sophisticated power strips have a master and slave socket arrangement, and when the "master" socket detects standby mode in the attached appliance's current it turns off the whole strip.

However, there can be problems detecting standby power in appliances that use more power in standby mode (such as plasma televisions) as they will always appear to the power strip to be switched on. When using a master–slave power strip, one way to avoid such problems is to plug an appliance with a lower standby wattage (such as a DVD player) into the master socket, using it as the master control instead.

A different power strip design intended to save energy uses a passive infrared (PIR) or ultrasonic sound detector to determine if a person is nearby. If the sensors don't detect any motion for a preset period of time, the strip shuts off several outlets, while leaving one outlet on for devices that should not be powered off. These so-called "smart power strips" are intended to be installed in offices, to shut down equipment when the office is unoccupied.

It is recommended that appliances that need a controlled shutdown sequence (such as many ink-jet printers) *not* be plugged into a slave socket on such a strip as it can damage them if they are switched off incorrectly (for example the inkjet printer may not have capped the print head in time, and consequently the ink will dry and clog the print head.)

Within Europe, power strips with energy-saving features are within the scope of the Low Voltage Directive 2006/95/EC and the EMC Directive 2004/108/EC and require a CE mark.

Power Strip, Socket Arrangement

In some countries where multiple socket types are in use, a single power strip can have two or more kinds of sockets. Socket arrangement varies considerably, but for physical access reasons there are rarely more than two rows. In Europe, power strips without surge suppression are normally single row, but models with surge suppression are supplied both in single and double row configurations.

If sockets on a power strip are grouped closely together, a cable with a large "wall wart" transformer at its end may cover up multiple sockets. Various designs address this problem, some by simply increasing the spacing between outlets. Other designs include receptacles which rotate in their housing, or multiple short receptacle cords feeding from a central hub. A simple DIY method for adapting problematic power strips arrangements to large "wall warts" is to use a three-way socket adapter to extend the socket above its neighbors, providing the required clearance.[6] The PowerCube adapter is arranged as a cube, meaning the adapters do not fight for space next to each other.[7]

Power Strip, Surge Protection and Filtering

Many power strips have built-in surge protectors or EMI/RFI filters: these are sometimes described as **surge suppressors** or **electrical line conditioners**. Some also provide surge suppression for phone lines, TV cable coax, or network cable. Unprotected power strips are often mistakenly called "surge suppressors" or "surge protectors" even though they may have *no ability to suppress surges*.

Surge suppression is usually provided by one or more metal-oxide varistors (MOVs), which are inexpensive two-terminal semiconductors. These act as very high speed switches, momentarily limiting the peak voltage across their terminals. By design, MOV surge limiters are selected to trigger at a voltage somewhat above the local mains supply voltage, so that they do not clip normal voltage peaks, but clip abnormal higher voltages. In the US, this is (nominally) 120 VAC. It should be borne in mind that this voltage specification is RMS, not peak, and also that it is only a nominal (approximate) value.

Mains electrical power circuits are generally grounded (earthed), so there will be a live (hot) wire, a neutral wire, and a ground wire. Low-cost power strips often come with only one MOV mounted between the live and neutral wires. More complete (and desirable) power strips will have three MOVs, connected between each possible pair of wires. Since MOVs degrade somewhat each time they are triggered, power strips using them have a limited, and unpredictable, protective life. Some power strips have "protection status" lights which are designed to turn off if protective MOVs connected to the live wire have failed, but such simple circuits cannot detect all failure modes (such as failure of a MOV connected between neutral and ground).

The surge-induced triggering of MOVs can cause damage to an upstream device, such as an uninterruptible power supply (UPS), which typically sees an overload condition while the surge is being suppressed. Therefore, it is recommended not to connect a surge-protected power strip to a UPS,[8] but instead to rely solely on surge protection provided by the UPS itself.

More-elaborate power strips may use inductor-capacitor networks to achieve a similar effect of protecting equipment from high voltage spikes on the mains circuit. These more-expensive arrangements are much less prone to silent degradation than MOVs, and often have monitoring lights that indicate whether the protective circuitry is still connected.

In the European Union, power strips with surge suppression circuits can demonstrate compliance with the (LVD) Low Voltage Directive 2006/95/EC [9] by complying with the requirements of EN 61643-11:2002+A1. The standard covers both the performance of the surge suppression circuit and their safety. Likewise, power strips with telecoms surge suppression circuits can demonstrate compliance with the LVD by complying with the requirements of EN 61643-21:2001.

Power Strip, Surge Protection and Filtering, Daisy Chaining and Surge Protection

Connecting MOV-protected power strips in a "daisy chain" (in a series, with each power strip plugged into a previous one in the chain) does not necessarily increase the protection they provide.[10] Connecting them in this manner effectively connects their surge protection components in parallel, in theory spreading any potential surge across each surge protector. However, due to manufacturing variations between the MOVs, the surge energy will not be spread evenly, and will typically go through the one that triggers first.

Daisy chaining of power strips (known in building and electric codes as multi-plug adapters or relocatable power taps), whether surge protected or not, is specifically against most codes. As an example, the International Code Council's *International Fire Code 2009 Edition* in 605.4.2 states, "Relocatable power taps shall be directly connected to permanently installed receptacles."

Power Strip, Overload Protection

Where the current rating of the socket outlet, plug and lead of the power strip is equal to the rating of the circuit breaker supplying the circuit concerned, additional overload protection for the power strip is unnecessary, since the existing circuit breaker will provide the required protection. However, where the rating of a socket outlet (and, hence, the plug and lead of the power strip) is less than the rating of the circuit breaker supplying the circuit concerned, overload protection for the power strip and its supply cable is necessary.

In the UK, standard BS 1363 plugs and sockets are rated at 13 A but are provided on circuits protected by circuit breakers of up to 32 A. However, UK Consumer Protection legislation requires that plug-in domestic electrical goods must be provided with plugs to BS 1363, which include a fuse rated at not more than 13 A. Hence, in the UK and in other countries using BS 1363 plugs, this fused plug provides overload protection for any power strip. The fuse must be replaced if the power strip is overloaded, causing the fuse to operate.

In Australia and New Zealand the rating for a standard socket outlet is 10 Amperes but these outlets are provided on circuits usually protected by circuit breakers of 16 or 20 A capacity. Also, it is possible to insert an Australian/NZ 10 A plug into socket outlets rated at up to 32 A.[11] Hence, all power strips sold in Australia and New Zealand with three or more 10A socket outlets are required to have overload protection so that if the total current drawn exceeds 10 A the inbuilt circuit breaker will operate and disconnect *all* connected devices. These power strips have a reset button for the circuit breaker, which is used to return the strip to service after an overload has caused it to trip.

Power Strip, Safety

Electrical overloading can be a problem with any sort of power distribution adapter. This is especially likely if multiple high-power appliances are used, such as those with heating elements, like room heaters or electric frying pans. Power strips may have a circuit breaker integrated to prevent overload. In the UK, power strips are required to be protected by the fuse in the BS 1363 plug. Some also feature a 13A BS1362 fuse in the socket end.

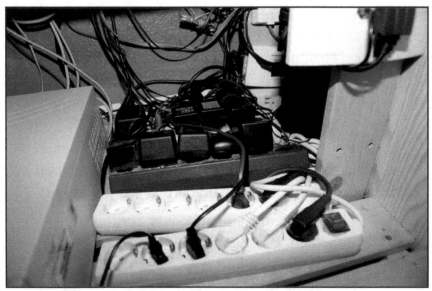

Multiple power strips and AC adapters

Power strips are generally considered a safer alternative to "double adapters", "two-way plugs", "three-way plugs", or "cube taps" which plug directly into the socket with no lead for multiple appliances. These low-cost adapters are generally not fused (although more modern ones in the UK and Ireland are). Therefore, in many cases the only protection against overload is the branch circuit fuse which may well have a rating higher than the adapter. The weight of the plugs pulling on the adapter (and often pulling it part way out of the socket) can also be a problem if adapters are stacked or if they are used with brick-style power supplies. Such adapters, while still available, have largely fallen out of use in some countries (although two- and three-way adapters are still common in the US, UK, and Ireland).

When plugging a device into a power strip, a buildup of carbon or dust can cause sparking to occur. This generally doesn't pose much of a risk in a non-explosive atmosphere, but explosive atmospheres (for example, near a gasoline refueling station or a solvent cleaning facility) require specialized explosion-proof sealed electrical equipment.

Power Strip, Safety, US Regulations

- Underwriters Laboratories standard 1363 contains requirements for *relocatable power taps*. Included in the scope section of the standard is the statement:

  > 1.1 These requirements cover cord-connected, relocatable power taps rated 250 V AC or less and 20 A AC or less. A relocatable power tap is intended only for indoor use as a temporary extension of a grounding alternating-current branch circuit for general use.

- National Electrical Code recognizes power strip as Multioutlet Assembly in Article 380.

Power Strip, Safety, EU and UK Regulations

In Europe, plugs and sockets without additional control or surge protection circuits are outside the scope of the Low Voltage Directive 2006/95/EC and controlled by National regulations, and therefore must not be CE marked. In the UK the legal requirements for plugs and sockets are listed in Statutory Instrument 1994 No. 1768, The Plugs and Sockets etc. (Safety) Regulations 1994.[12] This regulation lists the requirements for all domestic plugs and sockets; including socket outlet units (power strips), see[13] Electrical Equipment - Requirements for Plugs & Sockets etc. - Guidance notes on the UK Plugs & Sockets etc. (Safety) Regulations 1994 (S.I. 1994/1768).

The regulation requires all socket outlet units to comply with the requirements of BS 1363-2 Specification for 13A switched and unswitched socket-outlets and with the requirements of BS 5733 Specification for General requirements for electrical accessories. Sockets and socket outlets do not require independent approval under the regulations. Any plug fitted to the socket outlet unit must comply with the requirements of BS 1363-1 Specification for rewirable and non-rewirable 13A fused plugs. Plugs must also be independently approved and marked in accordance with the requirements of the regulation.

If a socket outlet unit contains additional control circuits or surge protection circuits they will fall within the scope of the Low Voltage Directive 2006/95/EC and must be CE marked. Socket outlet units with control circuits also fall within the scope of the EMC Directive 2004/108/EC.

Power Strip, History

Examples of power strips exist in the U.S. patent system dating back as far as 1929, starting with the creation of Carl M. Peterson's "Table Tap".[14] Another early example was created by Allied Electric Products in 1950.[15]

Perhaps the first modern designs for the power strip were created by the U.S. firm Fedtro, which filed two patents in 1970 for designs that hew close to designs used in the modern day.[16][17]

One early iteration, called a "power board", was invented in 1972 by Australian electrical engineer Peter Talbot working under Frank Bannigan, Managing Director of Australian company Kambrook. The product was hugely successful, however, it was not patented and market share was eventually lost to other manufacturers.[18]

Power Distribution Unit

A **power distribution unit (PDU)** is a device fitted with multiple outputs designed to distribute electric power, especially to racks of computers and networking equipment located within a data center.[1] Data centers face challenges in power protection and management solutions. This is why many data centers rely on PDU monitoring to improve efficiency, uptime, and growth.[2] For data center applications, the power requirement is typically much larger than a home or office style power strips with power inputs as large as 22 kVA or even greater. Most large data centers utilize PDUs with 3-phase power input and 1-phase power output. There are two main categories of PDUs: Basic PDUs and Intelligent (networked) PDUs or iPDUs. Basic PDUs simply provide a means of distributing power from the input to a plurality of outlets. Intelligent PDUs normally have an intelligence module which allow the PDU for remote management of power metering information, power outlet on/off control, and/or alarms. Some advanced PDUs allow users to manage external sensors such as temperature, humidity, airflow, etc.

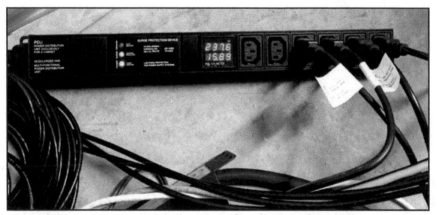

A rack mount PDU (sitting on the floor) that has surge protection and a digital display showing voltage (237.6) and amps (15.89).

Power Distribution Unit, Form Factors, Rack Mount

PDUs vary from simple and inexpensive rack-mounted

power strips to larger floor-mounted PDUs with multiple functions including power filtering to improve power quality, intelligent load balancing, and remote monitoring and control by LAN or SNMP.[1] This kind of PDU placement offers intelligent capabilities such as power metering at the inlet, outlet, and PDU branch circuit level[3]and support for environment sensors.[4]

Newer generation of intelligent PDUs allow for IP consolidation, which means many PDUs can be linked in an array under a single IP address. Next-generation models also offer integration with electronic locks, providing the ability to network and manage PDUs and locks through the same appliance.[5]

Power Distribution Unit, Form Factors, Cabinet

In data centers, larger PDUs are needed to power multiple server cabinets. Each server cabinet or row of cabinets may require multiple high current circuits, possibly from different phases of incoming power or different UPSs. Standalone cabinet PDUs are self-contained units that include main circuit breakers, individual circuit breakers, and power monitoring panels. The cabinet provides internal bus bars for neutral and grounding. Prepunched top and bottom panels allow for safe cable entry.[6]

Circuit Breaker

A **circuit breaker** is an automatically operated electrical switch designed to protect an electrical circuit from damage caused by excess current from an overload or short circuit. Its basic function is to interrupt current flow after a fault is detected. Unlike a fuse, which operates once and then must be replaced, a circuit breaker can be reset (either manually or automatically) to resume normal operation.

Circuit breakers are made in varying sizes, from small devices that protect low-current circuits or individual household appliance, up to large switchgear designed to protect high voltage circuits feeding an entire city. The generic function of a circuit breaker, or fuse, as an automatic means of removing power from a faulty system is often abbreviated as OCPD (Over Current Protection Device).

Circuit Breaker, Operation

All circuit breaker systems have common features in their operation, but details vary substantially depending on the voltage class, current rating and type of the circuit breaker.

The circuit breaker must first detect a fault condition. In small mains and low voltage circuit breakers, this is usually done within the device itself. Typically, the heating or magnetic effects of electric current are employed. Circuit breakers for large currents or high voltages are usually arranged with protective relay pilot devices to sense a fault condition and to operate the opening mechanism. These typically require a separate power source, such as a battery, although some high-voltage circuit breakers are self-contained with current transformers, protective relays, and an internal control power source.

220 Volt, 30 Amp circuit breakers; one per PDU (as pictured in the previous chapter).

Once a fault is detected, the circuit breaker contacts must open to interrupt the circuit; this is commonly done using mechanically stored energy contained within the breaker, such as a spring or compressed air to separate the contacts. Circuit breakers may also use the higher current caused by the fault to separate the contacts, such as thermal expansion or a magnetic field. Small circuit breakers typically have a manual control lever to switch off the load or reset a tripped breaker, while larger units use solenoids to trip the mechanism, and electric motors to restore energy to the springs.

The circuit breaker contacts must carry the load current without excessive heating, and must also withstand the heat of the arc produced when interrupting (opening) the circuit. Contacts are made of copper or copper alloys, silver alloys and other highly conductive materials. Service life of the contacts is limited by the erosion of contact material due to arcing while interrupting the current. Miniature and molded-case circuit breakers are usually discarded when the contacts have worn, but power circuit breakers and high-voltage circuit breakers have replaceable contacts.

When a high current or voltage is interrupted, an arc is generated. The length of the arc is generally proportional to the voltage while the intensity (or heat) is proportional to the current. This arc must be contained, cooled and extinguished in a controlled way, so that the gap between the contacts can again withstand the voltage in the circuit. Different circuit breakers use vacuum, air, insulating gas, or oil as the medium the arc forms in. Different techniques are used to extinguish the arc including:

- Lengthening or deflecting the arc
- Intensive cooling (in jet chambers)
- Division into partial arcs

- Zero point quenching (contacts open at the zero current time crossing of the AC waveform, effectively breaking no load current at the time of opening. The zero-crossing occurs at twice the line frequency; i.e., 100 times per second for 50 Hz and 120 times per second for 60 Hz AC.)
- Connecting capacitors in parallel with contacts in DC circuits.

Finally, once the fault condition has been cleared, the contacts must again be closed to restore power to the interrupted circuit.

Circuit Breaker, Arc Interruption

Low-voltage miniature circuit breakers (MCB) use air alone to extinguish the arc. These circuit breakers contain so-called arc chutes, a stack of mutually insulated parallel metal plates that divide and cool the arc. By splitting the arc into smaller arcs the arc is cooled down while the arc voltage is increased and serves as an additional impedance that limits the current through the circuit breaker. The current-carrying parts near the contacts provide easy deflection of the arc into the arc chutes by a magnetic force of a current path, although magnetic blowout coils or permanent magnets could also deflect the arc into the arc chute (used on circuit breakers for higher ratings). The number of plates in the arc chute is dependent on the short-circuit rating and nominal voltage of the circuit breaker.

In larger ratings, oil circuit breakers rely upon vaporization of some of the oil to blast a jet of oil through the arc.[4]

Gas (usually sulfur hexafluoride) circuit breakers sometimes stretch the arc using a magnetic field, and then rely upon the dielectric strength of the sulfur hexafluoride (SF_6) to quench the stretched arc.

Vacuum circuit breakers have minimal arcing (as there is nothing to ionize other than the contact material). The arc quenches when it is stretched a very small amount (less than 2–3 mm (0.08–0.1 in)). Vacuum circuit breakers are frequently used in modern medium-voltage switchgear to 38,000 volts.

Air circuit breakers may use compressed air to blow out the arc, or alternatively, the contacts are rapidly swung into a small sealed chamber, the escaping of the displaced air thus blowing out the arc.

Circuit breakers are usually able to terminate all current very quickly: typically the arc is extinguished between 30 ms and 150 ms after the mechanism has been tripped, depending upon age and construction of the device. The maximum current value and let-through energy determine the quality of the circuit breakers.

Circuit Breaker, Short Circuit

Circuit breakers are rated both by the normal current that they are expected to carry, and the maximum short-circuit current that they can safely interrupt. This latter figure is the **ampere interrupting capacity (AIC)** of the breaker.

Under short-circuit conditions, the calculated or measured maximum prospective short-circuit current may be many times the normal, rated current of the circuit. When electrical contacts open to interrupt a large current, there is a tendency for an arc to form between the opened contacts, which would allow the current to continue. This condition can create conductive ionized gases and molten or vaporized metal, which can cause the further continuation of the arc, or creation of additional short circuits, potentially resulting in the explosion of the circuit breaker and the equipment that it is installed in. Therefore, circuit breakers must incorporate various features to divide and extinguish the arc.

The maximum short-circuit current that a breaker can interrupt is determined by testing. Application of a breaker in a circuit with a prospective short-circuit current higher than the breaker's interrupting capacity rating may result in failure of the breaker to safely interrupt a fault. In a worst-case scenario, the breaker may successfully interrupt the fault, only to explode when reset.

Typical domestic panel circuit breakers are rated to interrupt 6 kA (6000 A) short-circuit current.

Miniature circuit breakers used to protect control circuits or small appliances may not have sufficient interrupting capacity to use at a panel board; these circuit breakers are called "supplemental circuit protectors" to distinguish them from distribution-type circuit breakers.

Kilowatt-hour

The **kilowatt-hour** (SI symbol: **kW·h** or **kW h**; commonly written as **kWh**) is a unit of energy equal to 3600 kilojoules (3.6 megajoules). The kilowatt-hour is commonly used as a billing unit for energy delivered to consumers by electric utilities.

Kilowatt-hour, Definition

The kilowatt-hour is a composite unit of energy equal to one kilowatt (kW) of power sustained for one hour. Expressed in the standard unit of energy in the International System of Units (SI), the joule (symbol J), it is equal to 3600 kilojoules (3.6 MJ).[1][2]

The hour is a unit of time listed among the non-SI units accepted by the International Bureau of Weights and Measures for use with the SI.[3] Its combination with the kilowatt, a standard SI unit, is therefore permitted within the standard.

Kilowatt-hour, Unit Representations

A widely used symbolic representation of the kilowatt-hour is "kWh", from the unit symbols of its component units, kilowatt and hour. It is commonly used in commercial, educational, and scientific publications and in the media.[4][5] It is also the usual unit representation in electrical power engineering.[6] This common representation does not comply with the style guide of the International System of

Units (SI).[3]

Other representations of the unit may be encountered:

- "kW·h" and "kW h" are less commonly used, but they are consistent with the SI. The SI brochure[3] states that in forming a compound unit symbol, "Multiplication must be indicated by a space or a half-high (centred) dot (·), since otherwise some prefixes could be misinterpreted as a unit symbol." This is supported by a voluntary standard[7] issued jointly by an international (IEEE) and national (ASTM) organization, and by a major style guide.[8] However, the IEEE/ASTM standard allows "kWh" (but does not mention other multiples of the watt-hour). One guide published by NIST specifically recommends against "kWh" "to avoid possible confusion".[9]
- The United States official fuel-economy window sticker for electric vehicles uses the abbreviation "kW-hrs".[10]
- Variations in capitalization are sometimes encountered: KWh, KWH, kwh, etc., which are inconsistent with the International System of Units.
- The notation "kW/h" for the kilowatt-hour is incorrect, as it denotes kilowatt per hour.

Kilowatt-hour, Electricity Sales

Electrical energy is typically sold to consumers in kilowatt-hours. The cost of running an electrical device is calculated by multiplying the device's power consumption in kilowatts by the operating time in hours, and by the price per kilowatt-hour. The unit price of electricity charged by utility companies may depend on the customer's consumption profile over time. Prices vary considerably by locality. In the United States prices in different states can vary by a factor of three.[11]

While smaller customer loads are usually billed only for energy, transmission services, and the rated capacity, larger consumers also pay for peak power consumption, the greatest power recorded in a fairly short time, such as 15 minutes. This compensates the power company for maintaining the infrastructure needed to provide peak power. These charges are billed as demand changes.[12] Industrial users may also have extra charges according to the power factor of their load.

Major energy production or consumption is often expressed as terawatt-hours (TWh) for a given period that is often a calendar year or financial year. A 365-day year equals 8,760 hours, so over a period of one year, power of one gigawatt equates to 8.76 terawatt-hours of energy. Conversely, one terawatt-hour is equal to a sustained power of about 114 megawatts for a period of one year.

Kilowatt-hour, Electricity Sales, Examples

An electric heater consuming 1000 watts (1 kilowatt), and operating for one hour uses one kilowatt-hour of energy. A television consuming 100 watts operating for 10 hours continuously uses one kilowatt-hour. A 40-watt electric appliance operating continuously for 25 hours uses one kilowatt-hour. In terms of human power, a healthy adult male manual laborer performs work equal to about one half of one kilowatt-hour over an eight-hour day.

Kilowatt-hour, Conversions

To convert a quantity measured in a unit in the left column to the units in the top row, multiply by the factor in the cell where the row and column intersect.

All the SI prefixes are commonly applied to the watt-hour: a kilowatt-hour is 1,000 Wh (kWh); a megawatt-hour is 1 million Wh (MWh); a milliwatt-hour is 1/1000 Wh (mWh) and so on. The kilowatt-hour is commonly used by electrical energy providers for purposes of billing, since the monthly energy consumption of a typical residential customer ranges from a few hundred to a few thousand kilowatt-hours. **Megawatt-hours** (MWh), **gigawatt-hours** (GWh), and **terawatt-hours** (TWh) are often used for metering larger amounts of electrical energy to industrial customers and in power generation. The terawatt-hour and **petawatt-hour** (PWh) units are large enough to conveniently express the annual electricity generation for whole countries and the world energy consumption.

Kilowatt-hour, Distinguishing Between Kilowatt-hours (Energy) and Kilowatts (Power)

Energy is the work performed; and power is the *rate of delivery* of energy. Energy is measured in *joules*, or *watt seconds*. Power is measured in *watts*, or *joules per second*.

For example, a battery stores energy. When the battery delivers its energy, it does so at a certain power, that is, the rate of delivery of the energy. The higher the power, the quicker the battery's stored energy is delivered. A higher power output will cause the battery's stored energy to be depleted in a shorter time period.

Kilowatt-hour, Distinguishing Between Kilowatt-hours (Energy) and Kilowatts (Power), Annualized Power

Electric energy production and consumption are sometimes reported on a yearly basis, in units such as megawatt-hours per year (MWh/yr) gigawatt-hours/year (GWh/yr) or terawatt-hours per year (TWh/yr). These units have dimensions of energy divided by time and thus are units of power. They can be converted to SI power units by dividing by the number of hours in a year, about 8766 h/yr.

Thus, 1 GWh/yr ≈ 114.08 kW.

Kilowatt-hour, Distinguishing Between Kilowatt-hours (Energy) and Kilowatts (Power), Misuse of Watts Per Hour

Many compound units for various kinds of rates explicitly mention units of time to indicate a change over time. For example: miles per hour, kilometres per hour, dollars per hour. Power units, such as kW, already measure the rate of energy per unit time (kW=kJ/s). Kilowatt-hours are a product of power and time, not a rate of change of power with time.

Watts per hour (W/h) is a unit of a *change* of power per hour, i.e. an acceleration in the delivery of energy. It is used to measure the daily variation of demand (e.g. the slope of the duck curve), or ramp-up behavior of power plants. For example, a power plant that reaches a power output of 1 MW from 0 MW in 15 minutes has a ramp-up rate of 4 MW/h. Hydroelectric power plants have a very high ramp-up rate, which makes them particularly useful in peak load and emergency situations.

Other uses of terms such as *watts per hour* are likely to be errors.

Cryptocurrency, References

1. *Andy Greenberg (20 April 2011). "Crypto Currency". Forbes. Archived from the original on 31 August 2014. Retrieved 8 August 2014.*
2. *Polansek, Tom (2 May 2016). "CME, ICE prepare pricing data that could boost bitcoin". Reuters. Retrieved 3 May 2016.*
3. *Allison, Ian (8 September 2015). "If Banks Want Benefits of Blockchains, They Must Go Permissionless". International Business Times. Archived from the original on 12 September 2015. Retrieved 15 September 2015.*
4. *Matteo D'Agnolo. "All you need to know about Bitcoin". timesofindia-economictimes. Archived from the original on 26 October 2015.*
5. *Sagona-Stophel, Katherine. "Bitcoin 101 white paper" (PDF). Archived from the original (PDF) on 13 August 2016. Retrieved 11 July 2016.*
6. *"Archived copy" (PDF). Archived (PDF) from the original on 18 December 2014. Retrieved 26 October 2014.*
7. *"Archived copy" (PDF). Archived (PDF) from the original on 3 September 2011. Retrieved 10 October 2012.*
8. *Pitta, Julie. "Requiem for a Bright Idea". Archived from the original on 30 August 2017. Retrieved 11 January 2018.*
9. *"How To Make A Mint: The Cryptography of Anonymous Electronic Cash". groups.csail.mit.edu. Archived from the original on 26 October 2017. Retrieved 11 January 2018.*
10. *Law, Laurie; Sabett, Susan; Solinas, Jerry (11 January 1997). "How to Make a Mint: The Cryptography of Anonymous Electronic Cash". American University Law Review. 46 (4). Archived from the original on 12 January 2018. Retrieved 11 January 2018.*
11. *Wei Dai (1998). "B-Money". Archived from the original on 4 October 2011.*
12. *"Bitcoin: The Cryptoanarchists' Answer to Cash". IEEE Spectrum. Archived from the original on 4 June 2012. Around the same time, Nick Szabo, a computer scientist who now blogs about law and the history of money, was one of the first to imagine a new digital currency from the ground up. Although many consider his scheme, which he calls "bit gold", to be a precursor to Bitcoin*
13. *Jerry Brito and Andrea Castillo (2013). "Bitcoin: A Primer for Policymakers" (PDF). Mercatus Center. George Mason University. Archived (PDF) from the original on 21 September 2013. Retrieved 22 October 2013.*
14. Bitcoin developer chats about regulation, open source, and the elusive Satoshi Nakamoto Archived 3 October 2014 at the Wayback Machine, PCWorld, 26 May 2013
15. Wary of Bitcoin? A guide to some other cryptocurrencies Archived 16 January 2014 at the Wayback Machine, ars technica, 26 May 2013
16. *"UK launches initiative to explore potential of virtual currencies". The UK News. Archived from the original on 10 November 2014. Retrieved 8 August 2014.*
17. *Lansky, Jan (January 2018). "Possible State Approaches to Cryptocurrencies". Journal of Systems Integration. 9/1: 19–31. doi:10.20470/jsi.v9i1.335. Archived from the original on 12 February 2018. Retrieved 11 February 2018.*
18. *"The Dictionary Just Got a Whole Lot Bigger". Merriam-Webster. March 2018. Archived from the original on 5 March 2018. Retrieved 5 March 2018.*
19. *Yang, Stephanie (31 January 2018). "Want to Keep Up With Bitcoin Enthusiasts? Learn the Lingo". The Wall Street Journal. Retrieved 25 October 2020.*
20. *Katz, Lily (24 May 2017). "Cryptocurrency Mania Goes Beyond Bitcoin". Bloomberg. Retrieved 25 October 2020.*
21. *Browne, Ryan (5 December 2017). "Bitcoin is not a bubble but other cryptocurrencies are 'cannibalizing themselves,' fintech exec says". CNBC. Retrieved 25 October 2020.*
22. *Kharif, Olga (15 January 2018). "These Digital Coins Soar (or Fall) With Bitcoin". Bloomberg. Retrieved 25 October 2020.*
23. *Hajric, Vildana (21 October 2020). "Bitcoin Surges to Highest Since July 2019 After PayPal Embrace". Bloomberg Law. Retrieved 25 October 2020.*
24. *Vigna, Paul (19 December 2017). "Which Digital Currency Will Be the Next Bitcoin?". The Wall Street Journal. Retrieved 25 October 2020.*
25. *Steadman, Ian (11 May 2013). "Wary of Bitcoin? A guide to some other cryptocurrencies". Ars Technica. Retrieved 19 January 2014.*
26. *Popper, Nathaniel (1 October 2017). "Understanding Ethereum, Bitcoin's Virtual Cousin (Published 2017)". The New York Times.*
27. *"Ethereum Upgrade Adds to Crypto Mania Sparked by Bitcoin's Surge". Bloomberg.com. 25 November 2020.*
28. *Popper, Nathaniel (27 March 2016). "Ethereum, a Virtual Currency, Enables Transactions That Rival Bitcoin's". The New York Times. Retrieved 25 October 2020.*
29. *Hajric, Vildana (28 August 2019). "Bitcoin's Surge Means Smaller Rivals May Be Due for Rallies". Bloomberg. Retrieved 25 October 2020.*
30. *Saad, Amena (8 July 2020). "TikTok Takes on Crypto With Dogecoin Soaring 40% in 24 Hours". Bloomberg. Retrieved 25 October 2020.*
31. *Casey, Michael, 1967- (16 July 2018). The impact of blockchain technology on finance : a catalyst for change. London, UK. ISBN 978-1-912179-15-2. OCLC 1059331326.*
32. *"Blockchains: The great chain of being sure about things". The Economist. 31 October 2015. Archived from the original on 3 July 2016. Retrieved 18 June 2016.*
33. *Badkar, Mamta (14 May 2018). "Fed's Bullard: Cryptocurrencies creating 'non-uniform' currency in US". Financial Times. Archived from the original on 15 May 2018. Retrieved 14 May 2018.*
34. "How Cryptocurrencies Could Upend Banks' Monetary Role". Archived 27 September 2013 at the Wayback Machine, *American Banker.* 26 May 2013
35. *Narayanan, Arvind; Bonneau, Joseph; Felten, Edward; Miller, Andrew; Goldfeder, Steven (2016). Bitcoin and cryptocurrency technologies: a comprehensive introduction. Princeton: Princeton University Press. ISBN 978-0-691-17169-2.*
36. *"Blockchain". Investopedia. Archived from the original on 23 March 2016. Retrieved 19 March 2016. Based on the Bitcoin protocol, the blockchain database is shared by all nodes participating in a system.*
37. *Iansiti, Marco; Lakhani, Karim R. (January 2017). "The Truth About Blockchain". Harvard Business Review. Harvard University. Archived from the original on 18 January 2017. Retrieved 17 January 2017. The technology at the heart of bitcoin and other virtual currencies, blockchain is an open, distributed ledger that can record transactions between two parties efficiently and in a verifiable and permanent way.*
38. *Raval, Siraj (2016). Decentralized Applications: Harnessing Bitcoin's Blockchain Technology. O'Reilly Media, Inc. pp. 1–2. ISBN 978-1-4919-2452-5.*
39. *Bedford Taylor, Michael (1 September 2017). "The Evolution of Bitcoin Hardware". Computer.*
40. *Hern, Alex (17 January 2018). "Bitcoin's energy usage is huge – we can't afford to ignore it". The Guardian. Archived from the original on 23 January 2018. Retrieved 23 January 2018.*
41. *Baraniuk, Chris (3 July 2019). "Bitcoin's global energy use 'equals Switzerland'". BBC News. Retrieved 2 February 2020.*
42. *"China's Crypto Crackdown Sends Miners Scurrying to Chilly Canada". Bloomberg L.P. 2 February 2018. Archived from the original on 4 March 2018. Retrieved 3 March 2018.*
43. *"Cryptocurrency mining operation launched by Iron Bridge Resources". World Oil. 26 January 2018. Archived from the original*

on 30 January 2018.

44. *"Bitcoin and crypto currencies trending up today - Crypto Currency Daily Roundup June 25 - Market Exclusive". marketexclusive.com. Retrieved 27 June 2018.*

45. *"Iceland Expects to Use More Electricity Mining Bitcoin Than Powering Homes This Year". Fortune. Archived from the original on 20 April 2018. Retrieved 25 March 2018.*

46. *"Bitcoin Mining Banned for First Time in Upstate New York Town". Bloomberg L.P. 16 March 2018. Archived from the original on 20 March 2018. Retrieved 20 March 2018.*

47. *"Bitcoin mania is hurting PC gamers by pushing up GPU prices". Archived from the original on 2 February 2018. Retrieved 2 February 2018.*

48. *"Graphics card shortage leads retailers to take unusual measures". Archived from the original on 2 February 2018. Retrieved 2 February 2018.*

49. *"AMD, Nvidia must do more to stop cryptominers from causing PC gaming card shortages, price gouging". Archived from the original on 2 February 2018. Retrieved 2 February 2018.*

50. *"Nvidia suggests retailers put gamers over cryptocurrency miners in graphics card craze". Archived from the original on 2 February 2018. Retrieved 2 February 2018.*

51. *Lee, Justina (13 September 2018). "Mystery of the $2 Billion Bitcoin Whale That Fueled a Selloff". Bloomberg. Archived from the original on 19 December 2018.*

52. *"What You Need To Know About Zero Knowledge". TechCrunch. Archived from the original on 20 February 2019. Retrieved 19 December 2018.*

53. *Greenberg, Andy (25 January 2017). "Monero, the Drug Dealer's Cryptocurrency of Choice, Is on Fire". Wired. ISSN 1059-1028. Archived from the original on 10 December 2018. Retrieved 19 December 2018.*

54. *"On the Instability of Bitcoin Without the Block Reward" (PDF). Retrieved 5 May 2020.*

55. *"Price Fluctuations and the Use of Bitcoin: An Empirical Inquiry" (PDF). Retrieved 5 May 2020.*

56. *"The Economics of Cryptocurrencies – Bitcoin and Beyond" (PDF). Retrieved 5 May 2020.*

57. *"Archived copy". Archived from the original on 26 October 2018. Retrieved 25 October 2018.*

58. *"Archived copy". Archived from the original on 19 October 2018. Retrieved 25 October 2018.*

59. *Scalability of the Bitcoin and Nano protocols: a comparative analysis (PDF), Blekinge Institute of Technology, 2018, retrieved 18 December 2019*

60. *Pervez, Huma; Muneeb, Muhammad; Irfan, Muhammad Usama; Haq, Irfan Ul (19 December 2018), "A Comparative Analysis of DAG-Based Blockchain Architectures", 2018 12th International Conference on Open Source Systems and Technologies (ICOSST), IEEE, pp. 27–34, doi:10.1109/ICOSST.2018.8632193, ISBN 978-1-5386-9564-7, S2CID 59601449*

61. *Bencic, Federico Matteo; Podnar Zarko, Ivana (26 April 2018), "Distributed Ledger Technology: Blockchain Compared to Directed Acyclic Graph", 2018 IEEE 38th International Conference on Distributed Computing Systems (ICDCS), University of Zagreb, pp. 1569–1570, arXiv:1804.10013, doi:10.1109/ICDCS.2018.00171, ISBN 978-1-5386-6871-9, S2CID 13741873*

62. First U.S. Bitcoin ATMs to open soon in Seattle, Austin Archived 19 October 2015 at the Wayback Machine, Reuters, 18 February 2014

63. *Commission, Ontario Securities. "CSA Staff Notice 46-307 Cryptocurrency Offerings". Ontario Securities Commission. Archived from the original on 29 September 2017. Retrieved 20 January 2018.*

64. *"SEC Issues Investigative Report Concluding DAO Tokens, a Digital Asset, Were Securities". sec.gov. Archived from the original on 10 October 2017. Retrieved 20 January 2018.*

65. *"Company Halts ICO After SEC Raises Registration Concerns". sec.gov. Archived from the original on 19 January 2018. Retrieved 20 January 2018.*

66. R Atkins (Feb. 2018). Switzerland sets out guidelines to support initial coin offerings Archived 27 May 2018 at the Wayback Machine. *Financial Times.* Retrieved 26 May 2018.

67. *Kharpal, Arjun (12 April 2017). "Bitcoin value rises over $1 billion as Japan, Russia move to legitimize cryptocurrency". CNBC. Archived from the original on 19 March 2018. Retrieved 19 March 2018.*

68. *"Regulation of Cryptocurrency Around the World" (PDF). Library of Congress. The Law Library of Congress, Global Legal Research Center. June 2018. pp. 4–5. Archived (PDF) from the original on 14 August 2018. Retrieved 15 August 2018.*

69. *Fung, Brian (21 May 2018). "State regulators unveil nationwide crackdown on suspicious cryptocurrency investment schemes". The Washington Post. Archived from the original on 27 May 2018. Retrieved 27 May 2018.*

70. Bitcoin's Legality Around The World Archived 16 September 2017 at the Wayback Machine, Forbes, 31 January 2014

71. *Tasca, Paolo (7 September 2015). "Digital Currencies: Principles, Trends, Opportunities, and Risks". Social Science Research Network. SSRN 2657598.*

72. *Thompson, Luke (24 August 2018). "Bank of Thailand to launch its own crypto-currency". Asia Times. Archived from the original on 27 August 2018. Retrieved 27 August 2018.*

73. *Matsakis, Louise (30 January 2018). "Cryptocurrency scams are just straight-up trolling at this point". Wired. Archived from the original on 1 April 2018. Retrieved 2 April 2018.*

74. *Weinglass, Simona (28 March 2018). "European Union bans binary options, strictly regulates CFDs". The Times of Israel. Archived from the original on 1 April 2018. Retrieved 2 April 2018.*

75. *Alsoszatai-Petheo, Melissa (14 May 2018). "Bing Ads to disallow cryptocurrency advertising". Microsoft. Archived from the original on 17 May 2018. Retrieved 16 May 2018.*

76. *French, Jordan (2 April 2018). "3 Key Factors Behind Bitcoin's Current Slide". theStreet.com. Archived from the original on 3 April 2018. Retrieved 2 April 2018.*

77. *Wilson, Thomas (28 March 2018). "Twitter and LinkedIn ban cryptocurrency adverts – leaving regulators behind". Independent. Reuters. Archived from the original on 4 April 2018. Retrieved 3 April 2018.*

78. *Rushe, Dominic (25 March 2014). "Bitcoin to be treated as property instead of currency by IRS". The Guardian. Archived from the original on 1 June 2016. Retrieved 8 February 2018.*

79. On the Complexity and Behaviour of Cryptocurrencies Compared to Other Markets, 7 November 2014

80. *"IRS has begun sending letters to virtual currency owners advising them to pay back taxes, file amended returns; part of agency's larger efforts | Internal Revenue Service". www.irs.gov.*

81. *Iwamura, Mitsuru; Kitamura, Yukinobu; Matsumoto, Tsutomu (28 February 2014). "Is Bitcoin the Only Cryptocurrency in the Town? Economics of Cryptocurrency and Friedrich A. Hayek". doi:10.2139/ssrn.2405790. hdl:10086/26493. S2CID 154268460. SSRN 2405790.*

82. ALI, S, T; CLARKE, D; MCCORRY, P; Bitcoin: Perils of an Unregulated Global P2P Currency [By S. T Ali, D. Clarke, P. McCorry Newcastle upon Tyne: Newcastle University: Computing Science, 2015. (Newcastle University, Computing Science, Technical Report Series, No. CS-TR-1470)

83. Mt. Gox Seeks Bankruptcy After $480 Million Bitcoin Loss Archived 12 January 2015 at the Wayback Machine, Carter Dougherty and Grace Huang, Bloomberg News, 28 February 2014

84. Sarah Jeong, DEA Agent Who Faked a Murder and Took Bitcoins from Silk Road Explains Himself Archived 29 December 2017 at the Wayback Machine, *Motherboard*, Vice (25 October 2015).

85. Nate Raymond, Ex-agent in Silk Road probe gets more prison time for bitcoin theft Archived 29 December 2017 at the Wayback Machine, Reuters (7 November 2017).

86. Cyris Farivar, GAW Miners founder owes nearly $10 million to SEC over Bitcoin fraud Archived 29 December 2017 at the

Wayback Machine, *Ars Technica* (5 October 2017).

87. Russell, Jon. *"Tether, a startup that works with bitcoin exchanges, claims a hacker stole $31M"*. TechCrunch. *Archived from the original on 21 November 2017. Retrieved 22 November 2017.*
88. Cimpanu, Catalin (4 September 2018). *"Bitcoin Gold delisted from major cryptocurrency exchange after refusing to pay hack damages"*. ZDNet.
89. Eric Lam, Jiyeun Lee, and Jordan Robertson (10 June 2018), *Cryptocurrencies Lose $42 Billion After South Korean Bourse Hack, Bloomberg News, archived from the original on 12 June 2018, retrieved 12 June 2018*
90. Roberts, Jeff John (9 July 2018). *"Another Crypto Fail: Hackers Steal $23.5 Million from Token Service Bancor"*. Fortune. *Archived from the original on 10 July 2018. Retrieved 10 July 2018.*
91. *"News releases AMF: 2018"*. The Autorité des marchés financiers (AMF). *15 March 2018. Archived from the original on 11 May 2018. Retrieved 10 May 2018.*
92. Raeesi, Reza (23 April 2015). *"The Silk Road, Bitcoins and the Global Prohibition Regime on the International Trade in Illicit Drugs: Can this Storm Be Weathered?"*. Glendon Journal of International Studies / Revue d'Études Internationales de Glendon. *8 (1–2). ISSN 2291-3920. Archived from the original on 22 December 2015.*
93. Polgar, David. *"Cryptocurrency is a giant multi-level marketing scheme"*. Quartz. Quartz Media LLC. *Archived from the original on 1 March 2018. Retrieved 2 March 2018.*
94. Analysis of Cryptocurrency Bubbles Archived 24 January 2018 at the Wayback Machine. *Bitcoins and Bank Runs: Analysis of Market Imperfections and Investor Hysterics.* Social Science Research Network (SSRN). Retrieved 24 December 2017.
95. McCrum, Dan (10 November 2015), *"Bitcoin's place in the long history of pyramid schemes"*, Financial Times, *archived from the original on 23 March 2017*
96. Kim, Tae (27 July 2017), *Billionaire investor Marks, who called the dotcom bubble, says bitcoin is a 'pyramid scheme'*, CNBC, *archived from the original on 5 September 2017*
97. Paumgarten, Nick (15 October 2018). *"The Prophets of Cryptocurrency Survey the Boom and Bust"*. www.newyorker.com. The New Yorker. Retrieved 20 August 2019.
98. Cryptocurrency and Global Financial Security Panel at Georgetown Diplomacy Conf Archived 15 August 2014 at the Wayback Machine, MeetUp, 11 April 2014
99. Schwartzkopff, Frances (17 December 2013). *"Bitcoins Spark Regulatory Crackdown as Denmark Drafts Rules"*. Bloomberg. *Archived from the original on 29 December 2013. Retrieved 29 December 2013.*
100. Sidel, Robin (22 December 2013). *"Banks Mostly Avoid Providing Bitcoin Services. Lenders Don't Share Investors' Enthusiasm for the Virtual-Currency Craze"*. The Wall Street Journal. *Archived from the original on 19 November 2015. Retrieved 29 December 2013.*
101. decentralized currencies impact on central banks Archived 4 March 2016 at the Wayback Machine, RTÉ News, 3 April 2014
102. Four Reasons You Shouldn't Buy Bitcoins Archived 23 August 2017 at the Wayback Machine, Forbes, 3 April 2013
103. Will 2020 Be The Year Cryptocurrency And Blockchain Becomes Operational?
104. Enabling the next wave of mainstream cryptocurrency adoption at NRF 2020
105. Foteinis, Spyros (7 February 2018). *"Bitcoin's alarming carbon footprint"*. Nature. *554 (7691): 169. Bibcode:2018Natur.554..169F. doi:10.1038/d41586-018-01625-x.*
106. Krause, Max J.; Tolaymat, Thabet (November 2018). *"Quantification of energy and carbon costs for mining cryptocurrencies"*. Nature Sustainability. *1 (11): 711–718. doi:10.1038/s41893-018-0152-7. ISSN 2398-9629. S2CID 169170289.*
107. Stoll, Christian; Klaaßen, Lena; Gallersdörfer, Ulrich (17 July 2019). *"The Carbon Footprint of Bitcoin"*. Joule. *3 (7): 1647–1661. doi:10.1016/j.joule.2019.05.012. ISSN 2542-4785.*
108. Want to make money off Bitcoin mining? Hint: Don't mine Archived 5 May 2014 at the Wayback Machine, The Week, 15 April 2013
109. Keeping Your Cryptocurrency Safe Archived 12 July 2014 at the Wayback Machine, Center for a Stateless Society, 1 April 2014
110. *"Scamcoins"*. August 2013. *Archived from the original on 1 February 2014.*
111. Bradbury, Danny (25 June 2013). *"Bitcoin's successors: from Litecoin to Freicoin and onwards"*. The Guardian. *Archived from the original on 10 January 2014. Retrieved 11 January 2014.*
112. Morris, David Z (24 December 2013). *"Beyond bitcoin: Inside the cryptocurrency ecosystem"*. Fortune. *Archived from the original on 27 January 2018. Retrieved 27 January 2018.*
113. *"PAUL KRUGMAN: Bitcoin is a more obvious bubble than housing was"*. *Archived from the original on 17 March 2018. Retrieved 16 March 2018.*
114. Krugman, Paul (26 March 2018). *"Opinion - Bubble, Bubble, Fraud and Trouble"*. The New York Times. *Archived from the original on 4 June 2018. Retrieved 17 March 2018.*
115. *"Warren Buffett: Cryptocurrency will come to a bad ending"*. CNBC. *Archived from the original on 19 March 2018. Retrieved 18 March 2018.*
116. Imbert, Fred (13 October 2017). *"BlackRock CEO Larry Fink calls bitcoin an 'index of money laundering'"*. *Archived from the original on 30 October 2017. Retrieved 19 November 2017.*
117. *"Introducing Ledger, the First Bitcoin-Only Academic Journal"*. Motherboard. *Archived from the original on 10 January 2017.*
118. *"Editorial Policies"*. ledgerjournal.org. *Archived from the original on 23 December 2016. Retrieved 24 September 2015.*
119. *"How to Write and Format an Article for Ledger"* (PDF). Ledger. *2015. doi:10.5195/LEDGER.2015.1 (inactive 15 January 2021). Archived (PDF) from the original on 22 September 2015.*
120. Mendoza, Ron (14 October 2019). *"UNICEF Blockchain Fund: First UN Organization To Accept Cryptocurrency Donations"*. IB Times]. Retrieved 14 October 2019.
121. *"UNICEF launches Cryptocurrency Fund"*. www.unicef.org.
122. *"Unicef now accepting donations through bitcoin and ether"*. the Guardian. 9 October 2019.

Cryptocurrency wallet, References

1. Roberts, Daniel (15 December 2017). *"How to send bitcoin to a hardware wallet (url=https://finance.yahoo.com/news/send-bitcoin-hardware-wallet-140141385.html"*. Yahoo! Finance.
2. Divine, John (1 February 2019). *"What's the Best Bitcoin Wallet?"*. U.S. News & World Report. Retrieved 12 March 2019.
3. Newman, Lily Hay (2017-11-05). *"How to Keep Your Bitcoin Safe and Secure"*. Wired. ISSN 1059-1028. Retrieved 2019-03-10.
4. *"European Blockchain Services Infrastructure (EBSI)"*. European Commission. Retrieved 24 July 2020.
5. Antonopoulos, Andreas (12 July 2017). *Mastering Bitcoin: Programming the Open Blockchain.* O'Reilly Media, Inc. ISBN 9781491954386. Retrieved 14 September 2017.
6. *"Bitcoin Wallets: What You Need to Know About the Hardware"*. The Daily Dot. 2018-11-20. Retrieved 2019-03-10.
7. *"Bitcoin Startup Predicts Cryptocurrency Market Will Grow By $100 Billion in 2018"*. Fortune. Retrieved 2019-02-15.
8. Graham, Luke (2017-07-20). *"$32 million worth of digital currency ether stolen by hackers"*. www.cnbc.com. Retrieved 2019-02-15.
9. Gutoski, Gus; Stebila, Douglas. *"Hierarchical deterministic Bitcoin wallets that tolerate key leakage"* (PDF). iacr.org. International Association for Cryptologic Research. Retrieved 2 November 2018.
10. Air-gap jumpers on cyber.bgu.ac.il

Mining pool, References

1. *"Individual mining vs mining pool". 2014-08-30. Archived from the original on 21 March 2015.*
2. Ittay Eyal with Emin Gün Sirer:"Majority is not Enough: Bitcoin Mining is Vulnerable Archived 2016-12-03 at the Wayback Machine" in the 18th International Conference on Financial Cryptography and Data Security(FC).2014
3. *Eyal, Ittay. "The Miner's Dilemma" (PDF). Cornell University. Archived (PDF) from the original on 2017-08-09. Retrieved 2017-05-23.*, In the IEEE Symposium on Security and Privacy (Oakland), 2015.
4. *Antonopoulos, Andreas M. (2014). Mastering Bitcoin. Unlocking Digital Cryptocurrencies. Sebastopol, CA: O'Reilly Media. p. 210. ISBN 978-1449374037. Archived from the original on 1 December 2016. Retrieved 7 January 2017.*
5. *Pedro., Franco (2015). Understanding bitcoin : cryptography, engineering and economics. Chichester, West Sussex: John Wiley & Sons. ISBN 9781119019145. OCLC 894170560.*
6. *Antonopoulos, Andreas (2017). Mastering Bitcoin: Programming the Open Blockchain. O' Reilly Media. ISBN 978-1491954386.*
7. *Rosenfeld, Meni (November 17, 2011). Analysis of Bitcoin Pooled Mining Reward Systems. arXiv:1112.4980. Bibcode:2011arXiv1112.4980R.*
8. *"The History of Bitcoin Mining Pools".*

Bitcoin network, References

1. *"Charts". Blockchain.info. Archived from the original on 3 November 2014. Retrieved 2 November 2014.*
2. *Nakamoto, Satoshi (24 May 2009). "Bitcoin: A Peer-to-Peer Electronic Cash System" (PDF). Retrieved 20 December 2012.*
3. *Barber, Simon; Boyen, Xavier; Shi, Elaine & Uzun, Ersin (2012). "Bitter to Better – how to make Bitcoin a better currency" (PDF). Financial Cryptography and Data Security. Springer Publishing. doi:10.1007/978-3-642-32946-3_29.*
4. *"Bitcoin boom benefiting TSMC: report". Taipei Times. 4 January 2014.*
5. *Biggs, John (8 April 2013). "How To Mine Bitcoins". Techcrunch.*
6. *Gimein, Mark (13 April 2013). "Virtual Bitcoin Mining Is a Real-World Environmental Disaster". Bloomberg Business. Bloomberg LP. Retrieved 22 April 2015.*
7. *"The magic of mining". The Economist. 13 January 2015. Retrieved 13 January 2015.*

Graphics processing unit, References

1. *Denny Atkin. "Computer Shopper: The Right GPU for You". Archived from the original on 2007-05-06. Retrieved 2007-05-15.*
2. *Barron, E. T.; Glorioso, R. M. (September 1973). "A micro controlled peripheral processor". MICRO 6: Conference Record of the 6th Annual Workshop on Microprogramming: 122–128. doi:10.1145/800203.806247. S2CID 36942876.*
3. *Levine, Ken (August 1978). "Core standard graphic package for the VGI 3400". ACM SIGGRAPH Computer Graphics. 12 (3): 298–300. doi:10.1145/965139.807405.*
4. *"Is it Time to Rename the GPU? | IEEE Computer Society".*
5. *"NVIDIA Launches the World's First Graphics Processing Unit: GeForce 256". Nvidia. 31 August 1999. Archived from the original on 12 April 2016. Retrieved 28 March 2016.*
6. *"Graphics Processing Unit (GPU)". Nvidia. 16 December 2009. Archived from the original on 8 April 2016. Retrieved 29 March 2016.*
7. *Pabst, Thomas (18 July 2002). "ATi Takes Over 3D Technology Leadership With Radeon 9700". Tom's Hardware. Retrieved 29 March 2016.*

Application-specific integrated circuit, References

1. *Barr, Keith (2007). ASIC Design in the Silicon Sandbox: A Complete Guide to Building Mixed-signal Integrated Circuits. New York: McGraw-Hill. ISBN 978-0-07-148161-8. OCLC 76935560.*
2. *"1967: Application Specific Integrated Circuits employ Computer-Aided Design". The Silicon Engine. Computer History Museum. Retrieved 9 November 2019.*
3. *"Lipp, Bob oral history". Computer History Museum. Retrieved 28 January 2018.*
4. *"People". The Silicon Engine. Computer History Museum. Retrieved 28 January 2018.*

Motherboard, References

1. *Miller, Paul (July 8, 2006). "Apple sneaks new logic board into whining MacBook Pros". Engadget. Archived from the original on October 4, 2013. Retrieved October 2, 2013.*

Central processing unit, References

1. *Kuck, David (1978). Computers and Computations, Vol 1. John Wiley & Sons, Inc. p. 12. ISBN 978-0471027164.*
2. *Weik, Martin H. (1955). "A Survey of Domestic Electronic Digital Computing Systems". Ballistic Research Laboratory.*
3. *Weik, Martin H. (1961). "A Third Survey of Domestic Electronic Digital Computing Systems". Ballistic Research Laboratory.*
4. *Thomas Willhalm; Roman Dementiev; Patrick Fay (December 18, 2014). "Intel Performance Counter Monitor – A better way to measure CPU utilization". software.intel.com. Retrieved February 17, 2015.*
5. *Liebowitz, Kusek, Spies, Matt, Christopher, Rynardt (2014). VMware vSphere Performance: Designing CPU, Memory, Storage, and Networking for Performance-Intensive Workloads. Wiley. p. 68. ISBN 978-1-118-00819-5.*
6. *Regan, Gerard (2008). A Brief History of Computing. p. 66. ISBN 978-1848000834. Retrieved 26 November 2014.*
7. *"Bit By Bit". Haverford College. Archived from the original on October 13, 2012. Retrieved August 1, 2015.*

Power supply unit, References

1. *Woligroski, Don (December 14, 2011). "Power Supply 101: A Reference Of Specifications". Tom's Hardware. Retrieved July 12, 2018.*
2. Edwin D. Reilly, *Milestones in Computer Science and Information Technology*, Greenwood Publishing Group, 2003

ISBN 1573565210, page 14

3. *"Apple Didn't Revolutionize Power Supplies". Retrieved October 11, 2017.*
4. *Torres, Gabriel (2008-03-15). "How Much Power Can a Generic 500 W Power Supply Really Deliver?". Hardwaresecrets.com. Archived from the original on 2008-05-11. Retrieved 2009-03-28. Our generic 500 W power supply died when we tried pulling 275 W from it, so the maximum amount of power we could extract was 250 W – half the labeled amount!*
5. *"Anatomy of Switching Power Supplies". Hardware Secrets. Archived from the original on 2015-04-10.*
6. ti.com
7. KA3511BS – Intelligent Voltage Mode PWM IC, *Fairchild Semiconductor Corporation, 2001*
8. *"EPS12V Power Supply Design Guide, v2.92" (PDF). enermax.cn.*
9. *"ATX12V Power Supply Design Guide, v2.01" (PDF). formfactors.org. Archived from the original (PDF) on 2009-11-22. Retrieved 2011-11-23.*
10. *"ATX12V Power Supply Design Guide, v2.2" (PDF). formfactors.org. Archived from the original (PDF) on 2008-09-20. Retrieved 2007-04-08.*
11. Power Supply Design Guide for Desktop Platform Form Factors Archived 2015-01-14 at the Wayback Machine (ATX12V specification v2.3)
12. *Nathan Kirsch (2005-03-30). Skyhawk PSU ATX12V & EPS12V Compliance. Legit Reviews. Retrieved 2009-09-24. On the front of the box it says "Triple Rails for +12V" and then goes on to say 'Intel ATX 12V Version 2.0 & EPS 12V Version 2.1'". It turns out from our investigation that the above power supplies do not meet the ATX12V or EPS12V standards as the packaging claims.*
13. *"OCZ GameXstream 700 W Power Supply, Hardware Secrets". Archived from the original on 2007-09-27. Retrieved 2008-04-20.*
14. *"Power Supply Fundamentals (page 3)". silentpcreview.com. Retrieved 2008-04-20.*
15. *"Fujitsu 12V only concept whitepaper" (PDF). Retrieved 2012-01-26.*[permanent dead link]
16. *"How Intel is changing the future of power supplies with its ATX12VO spec".*
17. *"Single Rail Power Supply ATX12VO Design Guide". Retrieved 2020-01-09.*
18. *"Single Rail ATX12VO (12V Only) Desktop Power Supply" (PDF). Intel.*
19. *Christoph Katzer (2008-09-22). "Debunking Power Supply Myths". AnandTech. p. 3. Retrieved 2014-10-07.*
20. *"Cooler Master UCP Product Sheet" (PDF). Cooler Master. 2008. Retrieved 2014-10-11.*
21. *Martin Kaffei (2011-10-10). "SilverStone Strider Plus – 500 W Modular Power". AnandTech. p. 4. Retrieved 2014-10-11.*
22. *Mpitziopoulos, Aris; June 2016, Igor Wallossek 09. "Picking The Right Power Supply: What You Should Know". Tom's Hardware. Retrieved 2020-11-01.*
23. *"What is PSU Efficiency and Why is it Important? | Velocity Micro Blog". Custom Gaming & Enthusiast PC Blog | Velocity Micro. 2019-06-12. Retrieved 2020-11-01.*
24. *Oklahoma Wolf (September 14, 2007), The Bargain Basement Power Supply Roundup, jonnyGURU.com, archived from the original on July 23, 2009, retrieved 2008-01-31*
25. *Rutter, Daniel (2008-09-27). "Lemon-fresh power supplies". dansdata.com. Retrieved 2008-09-28. The lemon-market in PC power supplies has now officially become bad enough that no-name generic "500W" PSUs may actually barely even be able to deliver 250 watts. A realistic constant rating for these units is more like 200 watts. So the capacity inflation factor's hit 2.5, and it's still rising.*
26. *"High-Performance Power Supply Units". Tom's Hardware. Archived from the original on 2012-12-16.*
27. *""Google plans to go carbon neutral by 2008" by Bridget Botelho 2007". Archived from the original on 2009-07-17. Retrieved 2009-05-12.*
28. *"Ecova Plug Load Solutions" (PDF). 80plus.org.*
29. *"Modern Form Factors: ATX And SFX - Power Supply 101: A Reference Of Specifications". Retrieved 2018-04-19.*
30. *"Modern Form Factors: EPS, TFX, CFX, LFX, And Flex ATX - Power Supply 101: A Reference Of Specifications". Archived from the original on 2018-04-12. Retrieved 2018-04-19.*
31. *Hellstrom, Jeremy (March 13, 2017). "Dual PSU fans; a revolutionary idea from Enermax?". PC Perspective.*
32. *Tyson, Mark (5 October 2016). "Enermax launches Revolution Duo dual-fan PSU range". Hexus.*
33. *"Choosing a Power Supply: Active vs. Passive PSU". PC Perspective. March 16, 2020.*
34. *"Fujitsu 250 W supply specification" (PDF). Retrieved 2012-01-26.*[permanent dead link]
35. *Gerow, Jon (2006-08-10). "Modular Power Supplies: The Reality of the Resistance". motherboards.org. Retrieved 2008-03-30.*
36. *parsec (2013-09-13). "SATA not detected after PSU change". forums.tweaktown.com. Retrieved 2019-08-15.*
37. *"Power Supplies TekSpek Guide - SCAN UK". scan.co.uk. Retrieved 2018-12-30.*
38. *Evenchick, Eric. "Hacking Dell Laptop Charger Identification". hackaday.com. Retrieved 2015-11-30.*
39. Evercase UK: Power Supply Measurements, retrieved 1 June 2016
40. *"In the World of Power Supplies, Don't Mistake MTBF for Life Expectancy" (PDF). batterypoweronline.com. June 2006. Retrieved 2014-06-29.*
41. *"M12 Power Supply Series". Seasonic. 2014-03-28. Retrieved 2014-06-29.*
42. *"MTBF: Misquoted and misunderstood" (PDF). xppower.com. 2011-03-21. Retrieved 2014-06-29.*
43. *John Benatti (2009-08-01). "MTBF and power supply reliability". electronicproducts.com. Retrieved 2014-06-29.*
44. *"Redundancy: N+1, N+2 vs. 2N vs. 2N+1". datacenters.com. 2014-03-21. Retrieved 2014-06-29.*
45. *"Power Supply Design Guide for Desktop Platform Form Factors, Revision 1.31" (PDF). Intel. April 2013. p. 26. Archived from the original (PDF) on October 21, 2014. Retrieved February 6, 2015.*
46. *"ATX Specification Version 2.1" (PDF). Archived from the original (PDF) on 2003-09-24.*
47. *"Untangling the wires: Getting to know your power supply". TechRepublic. 2001-06-26. Retrieved 2019-10-05.*
48. intel (formfactors.org): SFX12V Power Supply Design Guide, Version 2.3 Archived 2016-04-14 at the Wayback Machine, p. 19 (PDF; 366 kB) April 2003
49. *Murenin, Constantine A. (2007-04-17). Generalised Interfacing with Microprocessor System Hardware Monitors. Proceedings of 2007 IEEE International Conference on Networking, Sensing and Control, 15–17 April 2007. London, United Kingdom: IEEE. pp. 901–906. doi:10.1109/ICNSC.2007.372901. ISBN 1-4244-1076-2. IEEE ICNSC 2007, pp. 901–906.*

Overclocking, References

1. *Victoria Zhislina (2014-02-19). "Why has CPU frequency ceased to grow?". Intel.*
2. *Wainner, Scott; Richmond, Robert (2003). The Book of Overclocking. No Starch Press. pp. 1–2. ISBN 978-1-886411-76-0.*
3. *Wainner, Scott; Richmond, Robert (2003). The Book of Overclocking. No Starch Press. p. 38. ISBN 978-1-886411-76-0.*
4. *Wainner, Scott; Richmond, Robert (2003). The Book of Overclocking. No Starch Press. p. 44. ISBN 978-1-886411-76-0.*
5. *Stokes, Jon. "IBM's 500GHz processor? Not so fast...". Ars Technica.*
6. *Toon, John (20 June 2006). "Georgia Tech/IBM Announce New Chip Speed Record". Georgia Institute of Technology. Archived from the original on 1 July 2010. Retrieved 2 February 2009.*
7. *"AMD FX-8350 Breaks CPU Frequency World Record". Retrieved 2018-03-02.*
8. *"Extreme-Temperature Electronics: Tutorial – Part 3". 2003. Retrieved 2007-11-04.*

9. Wainner, Scott; Robert Richmond (2003). *The Book of Overclocking*. No Starch Press. p. 48. ISBN 978-1-886411-76-0.
10. *"overclocking with dry ice!"*. *TechPowerUp Forums*. August 13, 2009.
11. Cooling baths – ChemWiki. Chemwiki.ucdavis.edu. Retrieved on 2013-06-17.
12. *Cycles, cells and platters: an empirical analysis of hardware failures on a million consumer PCs (PDF). Proceedings of the sixth conference on Computer systems (EuroSys '11). 2011. pp. 343–356.*
13. *Tasiran, Serdar; Keutzer, Kurt (2001). "Coverage Metrics for Functional Validation of Hardware Designs". IEEE Design & Test of Computers. CiteSeerX 10.1.1.62.9086.*
14. *Chen, Raymond (April 12, 2005). "The Old New Thing: There's an awful lot of overclocking out there". Retrieved 2007-03-17.*
15. *Colwell, Bob (March 2004). "The Zen of Overclocking". Computer. Institute of Electrical and Electronics Engineers. 37 (3): 9– 12. doi:10.1109/MC.2004.1273994.*
16. Web page for a typical motherboard claiming overclocking support
17. UK Health and Safety Executive: Top 10 noise control techniques
18. Article ID: 310064 – Last Review: May 7, 2007 – Revision: 6.2 How to troubleshoot problems during installation when you upgrade from Windows 98 or Windows Millennium Edition to Windows XP
19. Microprocessor 3: Core Concepts - Hardware Aspects. Philippe Darche. John Wiley & Sons, 2020 - 240 pages. P.128. https://books.google.ru/books?id=XeQGEAAAQBAJ&pg=PA128&lpg=PA128&dq=power+wall+"quadratically"+power&source=bl&ots=sURSwftUSd&sig=ACfU3U05pSRKfDjz6CfSI94Yp2mbfizY9A&hl=ru&sa=X&ved=2ahUKEwjU0fShlLntAhUOt4sKHU0gAB0Q6AEwEHoECBMQAg#v=onepage&q=power%20wall%20"quadratically"%20power&f=false
20. Alt+Esc | GTX 780 Overclocking Guide

Operating system, References

1. *Stallings (2005). Operating Systems, Internals and Design Principles. Pearson: Prentice Hall. p. 6.*
2. *Dhotre, I.A. (2009). Operating Systems. Technical Publications. p. 1.*
3. Special purpose systems and general-purpose systems terms
4. *"Desktop Operating System Market Share Worldwide". StatCounter Global Stats. Retrieved 31 October 2020.*
5. *"Mobile & Tablet Operating System Market Share Worldwide". StatCounter Global Stats. Retrieved 31 October 2020.*
6. *"Strategy Analytics: Android Captures Record 88 Percent Share of Global Smartphone Shipments in Q3 2016". 2 November 2016. Archived from the original on 5 November 2016.*
7. Special purpose systems and general-purpose systems terms
8. Special-purpose operating system term
9. Lorch, Jacob R., and Alan Jay Smith. "Reducing processor power consumption by improving processor time management in a single-user operating system." Proceedings of the 2nd annual international conference on Mobile computing and networking. ACM, 1996.

Solid-state drive, References

1. *Whittaker, Zack. "Solid-State Disk Prices Falling, Still More Costly than Hard Disks". Between the Lines. ZDNet. Archived from the original on 2 December 2012. Retrieved 14 December 2012.*
2. *"SSD Power Savings Render Significant Reduction to TCO" (PDF). STEC. Archived from the original (PDF) on 2010-07-04. Retrieved October 25, 2010.*
3. *Kasavajhala, Vamsee (May 2011). "SSD vs HDD Price and Performance Study, a Dell technical white paper" (PDF). Dell PowerVault Technical Marketing. Archived (PDF) from the original on 12 May 2012. Retrieved 15 June 2012.*
4. *"Solid State Storage 101: An introduction to Solid State Storage" (PDF). SNIA. January 2009. Archived from the original (PDF) on June 10, 2019. Retrieved 9 August 2010.*
5. *"WD shows off its first hybrid drive, the WD Black SSHD". Cnet. Archived from the original on 29 March 2013. Retrieved 26 March 2013.*
6. *Patrick Schmid and Achim Roos (2012-02-08). "Momentus XT 750 GB Review: A Second-Gen Hybrid Hard Drive". Retrieved 2013-11-07.*
7. *Anand Lal Shimpi (2011-12-13). "Seagate 2nd Generation Momentus XT (750GB) Hybrid HDD Review". Archived from the original on 2013-11-01. Retrieved 2013-11-07.*
8. *"The Truth About SSD Data Retention". Archived from the original on 2017-03-18. Retrieved 2017-11-05.*
9. *"NF1 SSD | Samsung Semiconductor". Samsung.com.*
10. *"All-Flash NVMe Servers | Supermicro". SuperMicro.com.*

Advanced Micro Devices, Notes

1. *"AMD Reports Fourth Quarter and Annual 2020 Financial Results". Advanced Micro Devices. January 26, 2021. Retrieved January 28, 2021.*
2. The other founding members were Ed Turney, John Carey, Sven Simonsen, Jack Gifford and three members from Gifford's team: Frank Botte, Jim Giles, and Larry Stenger.
3. Rodengen, p. 30.
4. "Fairchild's Offspring". *Business Week*. August 25, 1997. p. 84.
5. Mueller, Scott. *Upgrading and Repairing PCs*. Que Publishing, 2013. p. 6.
6. Malone, Michael S. "Silicon Insider: AMD-Intel Feud Continues". *ABC News*. April 24, 2003.
7. Rodengen, p. 36.

Nvidia, References

1. *"NVIDIA Annual Reports 2020" (PDF). nvidianews.nvidia.com. Nvidia. December 2020.*
2. *"NVIDIA Corporation – Investor Resources – FAQs". investor.nvidia.com.*
3. *Clark, Don (August 4, 2011). "J.P. Morgan Shows Benefits from Chip Change". WSJ Digits Blog. Retrieved September 14, 2011.*
4. *"Top500 Supercomputing Sites". Top500. Retrieved September 14, 2011.*
5. *Burns, Chris (August 3, 2011). "2011 The Year of Nvidia dominating Android Superphones and tablets". SlashGear. Retrieved September 14, 2011.*
6. *"Tegra Super Tablets". Nvidia. Retrieved September 14, 2011.*

7.   *"Tegra Super Phones". Nvidia. Retrieved September 14, 2011.*
8.   Newman, Daniel. *"Nvidia will dominate this crucial part of the AI market for at least the next two years". MarketWatch. Retrieved September 20, 2020.*
9.   *"Company Info". Nvidia.com. Retrieved November 9, 2010.*

Overclocking, References

1.   *Victoria Zhislina (2014-02-19). "Why has CPU frequency ceased to grow?". Intel.*
2.   *Wainner, Scott; Richmond, Robert (2003). The Book of Overclocking. No Starch Press. pp. 1–2. ISBN 978-1-886411-76-0.*
3.   *Wainner, Scott; Richmond, Robert (2003). The Book of Overclocking. No Starch Press. p. 38. ISBN 978-1-886411-76-0.*
4.   *Wainner, Scott; Richmond, Robert (2003). The Book of Overclocking. No Starch Press. p. 44. ISBN 978-1-886411-76-0.*
5.   *Stokes, Jon. "IBM's 500GHz processor? Not so fast...". Ars Technica.*
6.   *Toon, John (20 June 2006). "Georgia Tech/IBM Announce New Chip Speed Record". Georgia Institute of Technology. Archived from the original on 1 July 2010. Retrieved 2 February 2009.*
7.   *"AMD FX-8350 Breaks CPU Frequency World Record". Retrieved 2018-03-02.*
8.   *"Extreme-Temperature Electronics: Tutorial – Part 3". 2003. Retrieved 2007-11-04.*
9.   *Wainner, Scott; Robert Richmond (2003). The Book of Overclocking. No Starch Press. p. 48. ISBN 978-1-886411-76-0.*
10. *"overclocking with dry ice!". TechPowerUp Forums. August 13, 2009.*
11. Cooling baths – ChemWiki. Chemwiki.ucdavis.edu. Retrieved on 2013-06-17.
12. *Cycles, cells and platters: an empirical analysis of hardware failures on a million consumer PCs (PDF). Proceedings of the sixth conference on Computer systems (EuroSys '11). 2011. pp. 343–356.*
13. *Tasiran, Serdar; Keutzer, Kurt (2001). "Coverage Metrics for Functional Validation of Hardware Designs". IEEE Design & Test of Computers. CiteSeerX 10.1.1.62.9086.*
14. *Chen, Raymond (April 12, 2005). "The Old New Thing: There's an awful lot of overclocking out there". Retrieved 2007-03-17.*
15. *Colwell, Bob (March 2004). "The Zen of Overclocking". Computer. Institute of Electrical and Electronics Engineers. 37 (3): 9–12. doi:10.1109/MC.2004.1273994.*
16. Web page for a typical motherboard claiming overclocking support
17. UK Health and Safety Executive: Top 10 noise control techniques
18. Article ID: 310064 – Last Review: May 7, 2007 – Revision: 6.2 How to troubleshoot problems during installation when you upgrade from Windows 98 or Windows Millennium Edition to Windows XP
19. Microprocessor 3: Core Concepts - Hardware Aspects. Philippe Darche. John Wiley & Sons, 2020 - 240 pages. P.128. https://books.google.ru/books?id=XeQGEAAAQBAJ&pg=PA128&lpg=PA128&dq=power+wall+"quadratically"+power&source=bl&ots=sURSwftUSd&sig=ACfU3U05pSRKfDjz6CfSI94Yp2mbfizY9A&hl=ru&sa=X&ved=2ahUKEwjU0fShlLntAhUOt4sKHU0gAB0Q6AEwEHoECBMQAg#v=onepage&q=power%20wall%20"quadratically"%20power&f=false
20. Alt+Esc | GTX 780 Overclocking Guide

Mains electricity, References

1.   *"Access to electricity (% of population)". Data. The World Bank. Retrieved 5 October 2019.*
2.   [1], How is electricity used in U.S. homes?, US Energy Information Administration, 21 April 2015, (retrieved 26 July 2015)
3.   [2], The Future of Electricity in Domestic Buildings – a review, Andrew Williams, 28 November 2015, (retrieved 26 July 2015)
4.   [3]*Electrical Inspection Manual, 2011 Edition*], Noel Williams & Jeffrey S Sargent, Jones & Bartlett Publishers, 2012, p.249 (retrieved 3 March 2013 from Google Books)
5.   [4]*17th Edition IEE Wiring Regulations: Explained and Illustrated*], Brian Scaddan, Routledge, 2011, p.18 (retrieved 6 March 2013 from Google Books)
6.   IEC-phase
7.   IEC-Neutral
8.   IEC-PE
9.   *Halliday, Chris; Urquhart, Dave. "Voltage and Equipment Standard Misalignment" (PDF). powerlogic.com. Archived from the original (PDF) on 11 March 2018. Retrieved 14 March 2014.*
10. *"Power plug, socket & mains voltage in Brazil". WorldStandards. Retrieved 27 November 2020.*
11. *"Voltage in Saudi Arabia - Electricity Supply and Power Quality Overview". Ashley-Edison (UK). Retrieved 27 November 2020.*
12. CENELEC Harmonisation Document HD 472 S1:1988
13. British Standard BS 7697: Nominal voltages for low voltage public electricity supply systems – (Implementation of HD 472 S1)
14. ANSI C84.1: American National Standard for Electric Power Systems and Equipment – Voltage Ratings (60 Hertz) Archived 27 July 2007 at the Wayback Machine, NEMA (costs $95 for access)
15. *"Voltage Tolerance Boundary" (PDF). PG&E. 1 January 1999. Archived (PDF) from the original on 10 November 2019. Retrieved 22 November 2019.*
16. CSA CAN3-C235-83: Preferred Voltage Levels for AC Systems, 0 to 50 000 V
17. *Hossain, J.; Mahmud, A. (29 January 2014). Renewable Energy Integration: Challenges and Solutions. Springer. p. 71. ISBN 978-9814585279. Retrieved 13 January 2018.*
18. *"Godalming: Electricity". Exploring Surrey's Past. Surrey County Council. Retrieved 6 December 2017.*
19. *Electricity Supply in the United Kingdom (PDF), The Electricity Council, 1987, archived from the original on 1 April 2017*
20. *"Milestones:Pearl Street Station, 1882". Engineering and Technology History Wiki. United Engineering Foundation. Retrieved 6 December 2017.*
21. Thomas P. Hughes, *Networks of Power: Electrification in Western Society 1880–1930*, The Johns Hopkins University Press,Baltimore 1983 ISBN 0-8018-2873-2 p. 193
22. *"Power plug, socket & mains voltage in Brazil". WorldStandards. Retrieved 27 November 2020.*

Ohm's law, References

1.   *Consoliver, Earl L. & Mitchell, Grover I. (1920). Automotive ignition systems. McGraw-Hill. p. 4. ohm's law current proportional voltage resistance.*
2.   *Robert A. Millikan and E. S. Bishop (1917). Elements of Electricity. American Technical Society. p. 54. Ohm's law current directly proportional.*
3.   *Oliver Heaviside (1894). Electrical papers. 1. Macmillan and Co. p. 283. ISBN 978-0-8218-2840-3.*
4.   Olivier Darrigol, *Electrodynamics from Ampère to Einstein*, p. 70, Oxford University Press, 2000 ISBN 0-19-850594-9.

Ampere, References

1. *Jones, Daniel (2011). Roach, Peter; Setter, Jane; Esling, John (eds.). Cambridge English Pronouncing Dictionary (18th ed.). Cambridge University Press. ISBN 978-0-521-15255-6.*
2. *Wells, John C. (2008). Longman Pronunciation Dictionary (3rd ed.). Longman. ISBN 978-1-4058-8118-0.*
3. *"ampere". Merriam-Webster Dictionary. Retrieved 29 September 2020.*
4. *"2. SI base units", SI brochure (8th ed.), BIPM, archived from the original on 7 October 2014, retrieved 19 November 2011*
5. SI supports only the use of symbols and deprecates the use of abbreviations for units."*Bureau International des Poids et Mesures" (PDF). 2006. p. 130. Retrieved 21 November 2011.*
6. *"2.1. Unit of electric current (ampere)", SI brochure (8th ed.), BIPM, archived from the original on 3 February 2012, retrieved 19 November 2011*
7. Base unit definitions: Ampere Archived 25 April 2017 at the Wayback Machine Physics.nist.gov. Retrieved on 28 September 2010.
8. *Bodanis, David (2005), Electric Universe, New York: Three Rivers Press, ISBN 978-0-307-33598-2*
9. *Draft Resolution A "On the revision of the International System of units (SI)" to be submitted to the CGPM at its 26th meeting (2018) (PDF)*
10. *"ampere (A)". www.npl.co.uk. Retrieved 21 May 2019.*
11. *The International System of Units (SI) (PDF) (8th ed.), Bureau International des Poids et Mesures, 2006, p. 144, archived (PDF) from the original on 5 November 2013.*

AC power plugs and sockets, References

1. *Smart Guide Wiring: step-by-step projects, Fran J. Donegan, Creative Homeowner Press, 2004, p.74 (retrieved 2 February 2012 from Google Books)*
2. *John Mellanby (1957). The History of Electric Wiring. London: Macdonald.*
3. *"Alert noting non-compliant power strips" (PDF). 2009. Archived from the original (PDF) on 6 March 2016. Retrieved 25 October 2019.*
4. *"Sri Lanka Sets National Standard for Plugs and Socket Outlets". Public Utilities Commission of Sri Lanka. Archived from the original on 2 April 2019. Retrieved 25 October 2019. Standardized on Type G; sale of non-compliant sockets is banned as of August, 2018, and buildings must re-wire by August, 2038.*
5. *James S. Jennings. "Army Sustainment: The Three Most Common Electrical Safety Issues in Deployed Environments". Archived from the original on 23 February 2015.*
6. *"Universal Sockets Are Unsafe". Interpower Corporation. Interpower. Retrieved 6 July 2018.*
7. *"Universal AC Outlet • Setup Guide" (PDF). Anaheim, CA: Extron Electronics. November 2017. 68-1638-01 Rev. F. Archived from the original (PDF) on 16 May 2018. Retrieved 21 May 2018.*
8. Using electricity on a campsite Camping and Caravanning Club
9. Electricity on European Campsites Camping and Caravanning Club (UK, so "European" means mainland Europe)
10. IEC 61558-2-5

Power cord, References

1. *Skalak, Richard; Chien, Shu (1987). Handbook of bioengineering. McGraw-Hill. ISBN 9780070577831.*
2. NEMA - Flexible Cords Section Archived 2011-11-03 at the Wayback Machine
3. Merle Henkenius; Popular Mechanics Dec 1987 How to Repair an Incandescent Lamp:Installing an in-line switch; p.130; [1] (retrieved 3/23/12)
4. *UL 62 (2010-05-18). "Flexible Cords and Cables". Retrieved 2017-01-25.*
5. *UL 817 (2001-03-16). "Standard for Cord Sets and Power-Supply Cords". Retrieved 2017-01-25.*

Power strip, References

1. *"Power Strip Buying Guide".*
2. *"Dan's Data - Power Conditioning". Dansdata.com. 2011-12-03. Retrieved 2012-03-09.*
3. *Dunn, Collin. ""Smart" Power Strips: Helping to Stop Idle Current Now!". Treehugger. MNN HOLDINGS. Retrieved 14 June 2013.*
4. *"BITS Energy Saving Smart Strip Surge Protectors". Bits Limited. Bits Limited. Archived from the original on 4 June 2013. Retrieved 14 June 2013.*
5. *Morris, Tyler. "Are Smart Power Strips Worth the Money?". Verde Energy Efficiency Experts. Verde Sustainable Solutions, L3C. Retrieved Feb 6, 2018.*
6. *"Power Adapter Outlet Liberator Method". Noprobo.com. 2008-12-24. Archived from the original on 2012-03-06. Retrieved 2012-03-09.*
7. *Rayner, Tristan (24 March 2015). "PowerCube – solving the problem of bad powerboards?". Techly. Retrieved 27 August 2015.*
8. *"APC Knowledgebase - using surge strips with UPS devices". Jpaa-en.apc.com. 2010-07-13. Archived from the original on 2012-07-31. Retrieved 2012-03-09.*
9. *"Official Journal of the European Union". Ec.europa.eu. Retrieved 2012-03-09.*
10. *"Surge Protection FAQs". 0051d9e.netsolhost.com. Retrieved 2012-03-09.*
11. *"Museum of Plugs and Sockets: Australasian heavy duty plugs and sockets". www.plugsocketmuseum.nl.*
12. *"Archived copy". Archived from the original on 2009-04-22. Retrieved 2009-06-28.*
13. *"Archived copy" (PDF). Archived from the original (PDF) on 2010-12-07. Retrieved 2009-06-28.*
14. *"Table tap". 1929-04-16.*
15. *"Extension cord tap". 1950-04-14.*
16. *"Multiple electric outlet bar". 1969-04-16.*
17. *"Multiple electric outlet unit". 1969-04-16.*
18. "Powerful patents", 17 Sep 2012, IP Australia.

Power distribution unit, References

1. *"Definition of: Power distribution unit". PCMag.com. Ziff Davis. Retrieved March 8, 2014.*

2.   *"Sentry Power Manager: Rack-Level Data Center Power Monitoring and Management". ServerTech.com. Server Technology. 2014. Retrieved January 1, 2015.*
3.   *"PDU Metering at the Inlet, Outlet, and Branch Circuits - Raritan". Raritan.com. 2015. Retrieved May 25, 2015.*
4.   *"Rack PDU - Rack Power Distribution - Intelligent PDU". Raritan.com. 2015. Retrieved May 26, 2015.*
5.   [1], Roth, Wayne D.; Donald A. Conner & Ronald S. Orris, "United States Patent: 9865109 - Systems and methods for controlling an electronic lock for a remote device"
6.   *"Cabinet Power Distribution". APC. Retrieved November 4, 2013.*

Circuit breaker, References

1.   Robert Friedel and Paul Israel, *Edison's Electric Light: Biography of an Invention*, Rutgers University Press, New Brunswick New Jersey USA,1986 ISBN 0-8135-1118-6 pp.65-66
2.   *""1920-1929 Stotz miniature circuit breaker and domestic appliances", ABB, 2006-01-09, accessed 4 July 2011".*
3.   *Flurscheim, Charles H., ed. (1982). "Chapter 1". Power Circuit Breaker Theory and Design (Second ed.). IET. ISBN 0-906048-70-2.*
4.   *Weedy, B. M. (1972). Electric Power Systems (Second ed.). London: John Wiley and Sons. pp. 428–430. ISBN 0-471-92445-8.*
5.   *"What is an MCB and how does it work?". Consumer Unit World. 16 September 2016.*
6.   https://www.eeweb.com/app-notes/solid-state-circuit-breaker
7.   John Matthews *Introduction to the Design and Analysis of Building Electrical Systems* Springer 1993 0442008740 page 86
8.   Hwaiyu Geng, *Data Center Handbook*, John Wiley & Sons,2014 page 542
9.   G R Jones (ed), *Electrical Engineer's Reference Book*, Butterworth - Heinemann Ltd, 1993, page 25/14
10.   A few manufacturers now offer a single-bottle vacuum breaker rated up to 72.5 kV and even 145 kV. See https://www.edu-right.com/full-knowledge-about-integrated[*permanent dead link*] Electrical Engineering in India, vol 157 issue 4 pages 13-23
11.   *"Siemens launches world's first 1200kV SF6 Circuit Breaker". Retrieved 14 November 2011.*
12.   *"ABB to develop ultra high voltage circuit breaker". Retrieved 14 August 2012.*
13.   *"High Voltage DC Switch Enables Supergrids for Renewable Energy, MIT Technology Review". Retrieved 19 July 2013.*
14.   *"Applications of Disconnecting Circuit Breakers, Michael Faxå, p.1" (PDF). Archived from the original (PDF) on 16 May 2013. Retrieved 9 July 2012.*
15.   *"HPL Disconnecting Circuit Breaker". Retrieved 9 July 2012.*
16.   *"Disconnecting Circuit Breakers, Buyer's and Application Guide, p. 10" (PDF). Retrieved 15 September 2014.*
17.   *"362 – 550 kV Disconnecting Circuit Breaker with FOCS: Small, smart and flexible, p.1". Retrieved 3 July 2013.*
18.   *"Switzerland: ABB breaks new ground with environment friendly high-voltage circuit breaker". Retrieved 7 June 2013.*
19.   *"Smart circuit-breakers for energy-efficient homes". The Economist. 2017-11-23. Retrieved 2018-01-15.*

Kilowatt-hour, References

1.   Thompson, Ambler and Taylor, Barry N. (2008). *Guide for the Use of the International System of Units (SI)* Archived June 3, 2016, at the Wayback Machine (Special publication 811). Gaithersburg, MD: National Institute of Standards and Technology. 12.
2.   "Half-high dots or spaces are used to express a derived unit formed from two or more other units by multiplication.", Barry N. Taylor. (2001 ed.) *The International System of Units*. Archived June 3, 2016, at the Wayback Machine (Special publication 330). Gaithersburg, MD: National Institute of Standards and Technology. 20.
3.   *"The International System of Units (SI)" (PDF). International Bureau of Weights and Measures (BIPM). 2019. p. 147. Retrieved 7 April 2020.*
4.   IEC Electropedia, Entry 131-11-58 Archived March 14, 2016, at the Wayback Machine
5.   See for example: *Wind Energy Reference Manual Part 2: Energy and Power Definitions* Archived November 26, 2007, at the Wayback Machine Danish Wind Energy Association. Retrieved 9 January 2008; "Kilowatt-Hour (kWh)" Archived March 2, 2016, at the Wayback Machine BusinessDictionary.com. Retrieved 9 January 2008; "US Nuclear Power Industry" Archived November 26, 2007, at the Wayback Machine www.world-nuclear.org. Retrieved 9 January 2008; "Energy. A Beginners Guide: Making Sense of Units" Archived November 26, 2007, at the Wayback Machine *Renew On Line (UK)*. The Open University. Retrieved 9 January 2008.
6.   ASTM SI10-10, IEEE/ASTM SI 10 American National Standard for Metric Practice, ASTM International, West Conshohocken, PA, 2010, [www.astm.org] "The symbols for certain compound units of electrical power engineering are usually written without separation, thus: watthour (Wh), kilowatthour (kWh), voltampere (VA), and kilovoltampere (kVA)"
7.   Standard for the Use of the International System of Units (SI): The Modern Metric System. (1997). (IEEE/ASTM SI 10-1997). New York and West Conshohocken, PA: Institute of Electrical and Electronics Engineers and ASTM. 15.
8.   *"10.57: Units derived from SI base units". The Chicago Manual of Style (17 ed.). Chicago: University of Chicago Press. 2017. Retrieved 1 April 2020.*
9.   *"Guide for the Use of the International System of Units (SI)" (PDF). National Institute of Standards and Technology. 2008. Retrieved 6 April 2020. Reference [4: ISO 31-0] suggests that if a space is used to indicate units formed by multiplication, the space may be omitted if it does not cause confusion. This possibility is reflected in the common practice of using the symbol kWh rather than kW·h or kW h for the kilowatt-hour. Nevertheless, this Guide takes the position that a half-high dot or a space should always be used to avoid possible confusion;*
10.   *"Electric Vehicles: Learn More About the New Label". fueleconomy.gov. US Department of energy. Retrieved 10 August 2014.*
11.   Average Price of Electricity to Ultimate Customers by End-Use Sector, U.S. Energy Information Administration, April 2018
12.   "Understanding Electric Demand" Archived June 6, 2016, at the Wayback Machine, National Grid
13.   *"The Board of Trade 1621-1970". Archived from the original on 2010.*
14.   *"Get enlightened about electricity". The Financial Express. December 20, 2004. Archived from the original on September 8, 2012. Retrieved 29 November 2009.*
15.   *"BHEL manufactured units generate record power". The Hindu. Press Trust of India. July 24, 2008. Archived from the original on November 7, 2012. Retrieved 29 November 2009.*

Proof of Work, References

1.   *Jakobsson, Markus; Juels, Ari (1999). "Proofs of Work and Bread Pudding Protocols". Secure Information Networks: Communications and Multimedia Security. Kluwer Academic Publishers: 258–272. doi:10.1007/978-0-387-35568-9_18.*
2.   *Dwork, Cynthia; Naor, Moni (1993). "Pricing via Processing, Or, Combatting Junk Mail, Advances in Cryptology". CRYPTO'92: Lecture Notes in Computer Science No. 740. Springer: 139–147. doi:10.1007/3-540-48071-4_10.*
3.   *"Cryptocurrencies and blockchain" (PDF). European Parliament. July 2018. Retrieved 29 October 2020. the two best-known –*

and in the context of cryptocurrencies also most commonly used

4. *Laurie, Ben; Clayton, Richard (May 2004). "Proof-of-work proves not to work". Workshop on the Economics of Information Security 2004.*
5. *Liu, Debin; Camp, L. Jean (June 2006). "Proof of Work can work - Fifth Workshop on the Economics of Information Security".*
6. How powerful was the Apollo 11 computer?, a specific comparison that shows how different classes of devices have different processing power.
7. *Abadi, Martin; Burrows, Mike; Manasse, Mark; Wobber, Ted (2005). "Moderately hard, memory-bound functions". 5 (2): 299–327.*
8. *Dwork, Cynthia; Goldberg, Andrew; Naor, Moni (2003). "On memory-bound functions for fighting spam". Advances in Cryptology: CRYPTO 2003. Lecture Notes in Computer Science. Springer. 2729: 426–444. doi:10.1007/978-3-540-45146-4_25. ISBN 978-3-540-40674-7.*
9. *Coelho, Fabien (2005). "Exponential memory-bound functions for proof of work protocols". Cryptology ePrint Archive, Report.*
10. *Tromp, John (2015). "Cuckoo Cycle; a memory bound graph-theoretic proof-of-work" (PDF). Financial Cryptography and Data Security: BITCOIN 2015. Lecture Notes in Computer Science. Springer. 8976: 49–62. doi:10.1007/978-3-662-48051-9_4. ISBN 978-3-662-48050-2.*
11. *Abliz, Mehmud; Znati, Taieb (December 2009). "A Guided Tour Puzzle for Denial of Service Prevention". Proceedings of the Annual Computer Security Applications Conference (ACSAC) 2009. Honolulu, HI: 279–288. CiteSeerX 10.1.1.597.6304. doi:10.1109/ACSAC.2009.33. ISBN 978-1-4244-5327-6. S2CID 14434713.*
12. *Back, Adam. "HashCash".* A popular PoW system. First announced in March 1997.
13. *Gabber, Eran; Jakobsson, Markus; Matias, Yossi; Mayer, Alain J. (1998). "Curbing junk e-mail via secure classification" (PDF). Financial Cryptography: 198–213.*
14. *Wang, Xiao-Feng; Reiter, Michael (May 2003). "Defending against denial-of-service attacks with puzzle auctions" (PDF). IEEE Symposium on Security and Privacy '03.*
15. *Franklin, Matthew K.; Malkhi, Dahlia (1997). "Auditable metering with lightweight security". Financial Cryptography '97. Lecture Notes in Computer Science. 1318: 151–160. doi:10.1007/3-540-63594-7_75. ISBN 978-3-540-63594-9.* Updated version May 4, 1998.
16. *Juels, Ari; Brainard, John (1999). "Client puzzles: A cryptographic defense against connection depletion attacks". NDSS 99.*
17. *Waters, Brent; Juels, Ari; Halderman, John A.; Felten, Edward W. (2004). "New client puzzle outsourcing techniques for DoS resistance" (PDF). 11th ACM Conference on Computer and Communications Security.*
18. *Coelho, Fabien (2007). "An (almost) constant-effort solution-verification proof-of-work protocol based on Merkle trees". Cryptology ePrint Archive, Report.*
19. *"Reusable Proofs of Work". Archived from the original on December 22, 2007.*
20. *"Cambridge Bitcoin Electricity Consumption Index". Cambridge Center For Alternative Finance. Retrieved 30 September 2020.*
21. Overview of the Bitcoin mining pools on blockchain.info
22. What is an ASIC miner on digitaltrends.com
23. *Vorick, David (13 May 2018). "The State of Cryptocurrency Mining".*
24. *Savva Shanaev, Arina Shuraeva, Mikhail Vasenin and Maksim Kuznetsov (2019). "Cryptocurrency Value and 51% Attacks: Evidence from Event Studies". The Journal of Alternative Investments. 22 (3): 65–77. doi:10.3905/jai.2019.1.081. S2CID 211422987.*

Proof of Stake, **References**

1. *"Cryptocurrencies and blockchain" (PDF). European Parliament. July 2018. Retrieved 29 October 2020.* the two best-known – and in the context of cryptocurrencies also most commonly used
2. *King, Sunny. "PPCoin: Peer-to-Peer Crypto-Currency with Proof-of-Stake" (PDF). Archived from the original (PDF) on 2017-12-11. Retrieved 2014-11-17.*
3. *Thompson, Jeffrey (15 December 2013). "The Rise of Bitcoins, Altcoins—Future of Digital Currency". The Epoch Times. Retrieved 29 December 2013.*
4. *Andrew Poelstra. "Distributed Consensus from Proof of Stake is Impossible" (PDF).*
5. *Vitalik Buterin. "On Stake".*
6. *"GitHub - ethereum/wiki: The Ethereum Wiki". August 7, 2019 – via GitHub.*
7. *"Resource exhaustion attacks on PoS". University of Illinois at Urbana–Champaign. 22 January 2019. Retrieved 15 February 2019.* resource exhaustion attack affecting 26+ several chain-based proof-of-stake cryptocurrencies. These vulnerabilities would allow a network attacker with a very small(in some cases, none) amount of stake to crash any of the network nodes running the corresponding software
8. *Buterin, Vitalik. "Slasher: A Punitive Proof-of-Stake Algorithm".*
9. *Buterin, Vitalik. "Slasher Ghost, and Other Developments in Proof of Stake". Retrieved 23 January 2016.* one thing has become clear: proof of stake is non-trivial
10. *Wood, Gavin. "Ethereum: A Secure Decentralised Generalised Transaction Ledger" (PDF). Retrieved 23 January 2016.* Ethash is the planned PoW algorithm for Ethereum 1.0
11. *"Nxt Whitepaper: History Attack". Nxtwiki. Archived from the original on 3 February 2015. Retrieved 2 January 2015.*